The End of the Job Description

Shifting from a Job-Focus to a Performance-Focus

The End of the Job Description

Tim Baker
WINNERS-at-WORK Pty Ltd

First published 2016 by
PALGRAVE MACMILLAN

Palgrave Macmillan in the UK is an imprint of Macmillan Publishers Limited, registered in England, company number 785998, of Houndmills, Basingstoke, Hampshire RG21 6XS.

Palgrave Macmillan in the US is a division of St Martin's Press LLC, 175 Fifth Avenue, New York, NY 10010.

Palgrave Macmillan is the global academic imprint of the above companies and has companies and representatives throughout the world.

Palgrave® and Macmillan® are registered trademarks in the United States, the United Kingdom, Europe and other countries.

ISBN 978–1–137–58144–0

This book is printed on paper suitable for recycling and made from fully managed and sustained forest sources. Logging, pulping and manufacturing processes are expected to conform to the environmental regulations of the country of origin.

A catalogue record for this book is available from the British Library.

A catalog record for this book is available from the Library of Congress.

Typeset by MPS Limited, Chennai, India.

This book is dedicated to Dr John H. Day, AM, a prominent and forward-thinking educationalist, who has had a positive impact on my life.

About the Author

Dr Tim Baker is a thought leader, international consultant, and successful author (www.winnersatwork.com.au). Tim was recently voted as one of *The 50 Most Talented Global Training & Development Leaders* by the World HRD Congress, which is awarded by a distinguished international panel of professionals "who are doing extraordinary work" in the field of HRD. He is the author of *The 8 Values of Highly Productive Companies: Creating Wealth from a New Employment Relationship* (Australian Academic Press), *The End of the Performance Review: A New Approach to Appraising Employee Performance* (Palgrave Macmillan), *Attracting and Retaining Talent: Becoming an Employer of Choice* (Palgrave Macmillan), *The New Influencing Toolkit: Capabilities for Communicating with Influence* (Palgrave Macmillan), and co-author with Aubrey Warren of *Conversations at Work: Promoting a Culture of Conversation in the Changing Workplace* (Palgrave Macmillan). Tim has conducted over 2430 seminars, workshops and keynote addresses to over 45,000 people in 11 countries across 21 industry groups and regularly writes for HR industry press.

Tim can be contacted at tim@winnersatwork.com.au.

Contents

List of Figures and Tables

Figures

Tables

Introduction

The job description – like the performance review – is a relic of the last century. Yet we still cling onto this antiquated Human Resource Management (HRM) tool in the hope that it aids employee performance. But we get frustrated with the job description, don't we? We are constantly tinkering with its format and content, hoping to make it more reflective of the work people are supposed to do in the organization. Instead of fiddling with the job description and asking how can we make it be more effective, we ought to be asking a better question: Is it still relevant? The answer is no, the job description is not relevant; it's past its "use by date." It's time to assign it to the industrial dustbin and replace it with something else. But what? What can we replace the antediluvian job description with?

The alternative to the job description – I believe – is the role description. Is it just another label for the same thing, you might be thinking. Is it old wine in new bottles? No. The role description is significantly different; it reflects a shift from a focus on the job to a focus on performance. What's more, the role description better captures work in the 21st-century workplace.

The job description – as its name suggests – is based exclusively on the characteristics of a specific job. A job, as we know, is typically broken down into six to eight job-related tasks, functions, or Key Result Areas (KRAs). The job description continues to be defined by the technical requirements of a particular job.

Therefore it neglects – or at best gives mere lip service to – key non-job competencies, such as being able to work in teams. This means the work document is incomplete and so, deficient. Organizational performance is much more than successfully completing the sum total of the technical requirements in the job description. Yet we are so dependent on the job description for most human resource management practices. A more complete performance model, factoring in job and non-job dimensions, is long overdue. Why isn't a comprehensive performance model common practice? I think the truth is that the continual concentration on the more measurable task-based job requirements is about maintaining a legally defensible performance appraisal system.

Legal or otherwise, the spotlight has been squarely on the performance of job-specific tasks for over two centuries. Nevertheless, non-job work has become more and more relevant to organizational performance. But non-job roles are not embedded in the job description to the same extent as the job-related tasks. The conventional job description fails to sufficiently capture what is expected of the incumbent in their non-job roles.

The role description better encapsulates the totality of work performance. Although the job description has evolved over time, it still is pretty much centered on the job; it's too hooked on the task-related activity of work. Put simply, the job description is too focused on the job and not enough on the individual doing the job. Some effort has gone into addressing this imbalance of job over non-job roles. Nonetheless, the job description is still too job-centric.

Advances in the job description have – to some extent – placed more emphasis on the job-holder's attributes. Most job description templates now have a competency-based component. The competency-based part typically describes the competencies needed to successfully perform job-tasks. But this realignment doesn't go far enough. Even considering the competencies necessary to execute the tasks of a job, the job description doesn't tackle competencies beyond the scope of the job; that is, organizational responsibilities. And if the job description does include organizational responsibilities, it's not usually as clear and unambiguous as the task competencies.

These organizational responsibilities are non-job roles; they cover a vast array of behaviors that can be productive or unproductive, helpful or unhelpful, constructive or destructive. Some non-job roles, as I mentioned before, are more critical in some industries than others. But overall, if executed well, non-job behaviors add to performance in all industries. I include four such roles in *The End of the Job Description*. This non-job roles framework, consisting of four non-job roles, is increasingly an important factor in the achievement of work in the 21st century.

The non-job roles framework – covering the roles, elements of the role, associated Key Performance Indicators (KPIs), and their targets – is the missing dimension in the job description. Although absent, or under-developed, the non-job dimension of work is a key factor in enterprise performance. Therefore *The End of the Job Description* explores this work dimension, focusing on the totality of work performance beyond the narrower job-focus.

Organizational performance – and the contributing performance of employees – is more dependent on the four non-job roles I cover in this book. Yet these non-job roles are not spelt out in detail in the job description. What's more, if these four non-job roles are not being performed by most employees to a high standard, several negative consequences will inevitably emerge in the workplace.

For instance, a widespread lack of enthusiasm and the absence of a positive attitude will adversely affect job satisfaction, attraction and retention, employee engagement, morale, and so on. Or, an organization filled with individuals who are not "team players" results in communication barriers in the form of silos and cross-functional communication breakdowns. Communication that is kaput because of no team work means that pretty soon, the product or service quality suffers; customers become unhappy.

Or, an organization filled with employees who have stopped growing and developing results in a stagnating business; worse still: a business going backward as their competitors progress. Likewise, a company populated with employees lacking interest in improving the business's efficiency or effectiveness, will severely limit its competitive edge in a hyper-competitive marketplace. While we have an implicit expectation that employees should perform these non-job roles, the job description bypasses them, or if they are mentioned, they are stated in generalities without specific KPIs and targets.

But the reality is this: If these four non-job roles are not performed by most employees, most of the time, any organization in any industry is in severe trouble. No amount of technical proficiency or know-how will compensate for chronic underperformance in these non-job roles. What is the point of employing someone who is technically proficient if they have a poor attitude, can't function in a team, choose to stop growing and developing, and don't want to help improve the way the business functions? Being technically capable is of little recompense if an employee can't or won't fulfill their organizational responsibilities. Performing at work extends beyond the bounds of the archetypal job description.

Since the Industrial Revolution, employees have been expected to play multiple roles at work; the concept of non-job roles is not new. But with work transformation, superior non-job performance can provide an enterprise (and employee) with a competitive edge. To be clear: I'm not suggesting that technical competence – the task-related dimension of a job – is any less relevant to performance. What I am saying is: The non-task-related roles that employees play or don't play are more imperative to the productivity of the 21st-century organization. This claim of mine is the basis for replacing the job description with the role description. The role description I'm promoting elevates the status of several key non-job roles. Briefly, the role description incorporates two dimensions of work – the job and non-job dimension.

More specifically, the role description has three components. One component is a continuation of the task-specific description of what the job-holder should do to successfully fulfill their job requirements. Assuming the job tasks are expressed clearly, accurately, and comprehensively, this information is already accessible in a well-crafted job description. The second component is an accompanying set of competencies the job-holder needs to master the job tasks. It is now common practice for the job description to have these two characteristics.

It is the third component that defines the difference between the job and role description. The third characteristic is the non-job dimension spelt out in detail. The inclusion of this third component adds to the job role – consisting of the first two components – and the non-job roles employees are increasingly expected to perform. By taking on board job and non-job roles in the one work document, the role description characterizes organizational work as a series of roles, rather than a single job.

Furthermore, by replacing the job description with a role description, the tasks of a job are calibrated as one of five work-related roles. As I pointed out before, this doesn't in any way lessen the significance or value of the technical dimension of work. More importantly, it elevates the significance and value of several essential non-job roles employees are tacitly expected to perform in the workplace.

Many organizations are using a *role profile* to explain what is expected of an employee in their workplace. But – as I see it – there are three problems with using a role profile, despite its inclusion heading in the right direction. First, the role profile is often written as an appendage to the job description; it is often not integrated into a single work document. So the role profile can be – and often is – viewed by the job-holder as an "add on" to the "important" information contained in the job description.

Second, the role profile usually covers job-related behaviors or competencies; it doesn't necessarily identify and spell out the non-job roles I have mentioned. The role profile is more often than not a collection of personal attributes the job-holder is expected to demonstrate in their job. Further, the role profile doesn't necessarily cover the roles of attitude and enthusiasm, working in a team, career development, and innovation and continuous improvement; the four roles in my non-job roles framework.

And third, the role profile doesn't usually contain KPIs or performance targets. We rationalize that non-roles, such as the four I just mentioned, are too subjective and therefore can't be measured with validity and reliability, don't we? It is therefore unsurprising that these non-job roles rarely, if ever, get discussed at performance appraisal time. And this lack of attention from managers reminds employees that non-job roles are less important than the task-specific aspects of the job. Predictably, the impact is that a non-job role – whether it is mentioned in the role profile or not – is *nice to have* rather than *must have*.

This by-and-large makes the role profile an attachment to the job description; a waste of time and of little consequence. For these three reasons, I propose a new approach that melds job and non-job roles into a single document I call a role description.

The End of the Job Description is broken into three parts. In Part I, I argue the case further; that we advance from the job description to the role description. I position the role description as the next generation work document. Further, the role description I'm promoting encompasses work performance, not just job performance. The job description – borne out of the traditional employment relationship, characterized as a "them and us" relationship – reinforces the old adversarial working relationship between employer and employee. As a worthy alternative, the role description is more suited to fostering a new psychological contract between individual and organization.

Part II describes in detail four important non-job roles. It begins with a rationale for the rising relevance of non-job dimension of work for performance. Subsequently, four chapters are devoted to each of the non-job roles in the framework. I have no doubt there are many other non-job roles that impact performance beside the four I cover. But I believe the four non-job roles covered in this book are universally applicable in all industries, and therefore, easily justified for inclusion in any performance management framework. These four non-job roles are integral to the changing world of work. Each non-job role is defined and broken down into a series of elements. Each element has ten KPIs as benchmarks for evaluating the employee's non-job role performance.

Part III is about implementation; how can the role description be entrenched in an organizational setting? I suggest several collaborative strategies you might like to try for crafting role descriptions. I then offer a methodology for evaluating non-job roles based on the KPIs outlined earlier in Part II. In the final chapter, I put the role description into the context of a performance management framework.

Thank you for reading my book; I hope you find it inspiring and practical.

part I

Job Descriptions to
Role Descriptions

chapter 1

Role Descriptions:
The Next Generation

It is timely to expand the predominantly restricted task-centric document that defines the specific requirements of a job. We should take on a more expansive model of work that goes beyond the skills, knowledge, and attitude necessary to do a particular job.

John sat down with Peter to conduct his dreaded annual performance appraisal. John was anxious about this interview since he had some concerns about Peter's performance. He wasn't too sure how Peter would react. In particular, John was concerned about four aspects of Peter's work. Specifically, his concerns were Peter's lack of initiative, his poor interpersonal relationships with others he worked closely with, his lack of commitment to developing his skills-set, and his general negative attitude. John was satisfied with the tasks that Peter was performing in his job. But basically John didn't think that Peter was performing his organizational roles. He had prepared thoroughly for the interview with several examples to back up his concerns.

As Peter took his seat in John's office, John noticed that Peter had a copy of his job description clutched in his hands.

John got straight to the point, "Peter, I think you are doing your job well in lots of areas, but there are four areas I am concerned about." "What are they?" said Peter defensively. "Well firstly, I am concerned that you don't show enough initiative in carrying out your work. For example, on Monday you complained to me that you are short-staffed. However, I noticed that you were doing tasks that you could have delegated to other people. You need to show more initiative and do things differently," said John decisively. "But nowhere on my job description does it mention the need to be innovative," Peter fired back.

After an awkward pause, John continued, "And the other day, you didn't help out in the production area when you finished your work load. That's not being a team player in my book." "It might be in your book, John, but once again, being a team player is not stated on my job description anywhere," Peter said, in a challenging tone of voice.

"Also, I have been trying for months to get you to do that new course on report writing. You keep telling me that you've been too busy. Apart from anything else, Peter, it would help you develop your career skills," said John, trying to appeal to John's self-interest. "I don't see developing my career skills written down anywhere on this job description," said Peter, looking down at the two-page document in front of him.

Plowing on, "I am also concerned that in the team meeting on Monday your attitude to the suggestions of others was pretty negative. I need you to display a more positive attitude around your work colleagues," John asserted. "Where is being positive and nice to people written in this document?" challenged Peter.

John thought to himself that these job descriptions were a waste of time. He further thought: Surely there must be a better way to get Peter to focus on performance in his role?

It is quite amusing, isn't it, that most job descriptions contain that all-too-familiar disclaimer at the end of the document that says the employee must perform *any other duties assigned by the supervisor.* This legal qualification implies that the job description fails to capture all the work requirements the employee is expected to perform. It is hard to imagine a worker on the assembly line of the Ford Motor Company needing this kind of legal disclaimer. In those days, jobs were very specific and clearly defined. What was expected of workers in those work-settings was very apparent and task-specific.

However, since the early part of the last century, the nature of work has changed profoundly. Work is now more multifaceted, the boundaries around the responsibilities of employees are ambiguous, and indicators of performance are different. Instead of accommodating the magnitude of these changes in work and their impact on employees and organizations, we have merely tagged a legal rider at the bottom of the job description to cover all bases. This has resulted in Dilbert-like jokes about the worth and value of the job description.

There are inevitably many challenges in crafting the ideal job description. I know this, having spoken with clients across 21 industry groups. A recent survey by The Creative Group polled advertising and marketing executives on the greatest challenge in writing job descriptions. When asked what the top challenge was in formulating job descriptions, 28 per cent of respondents said it was the identification of the necessary soft skills for the job (competency-based approach). On the other hand, 24 per cent claimed it was most difficult to accurately describe job duties (task-based approach).[1] Although *The End of the Job Description* is not a prescriptive text on how to address these two issues specifically, it will hopefully provide you with a better perspective on formulating a more comprehensive and contemporary analysis of the work that 21st-century employees are expected to perform.

The job description: the pillar of human resource management

Despite the fact that the essence of work has advanced beyond the usefulness of the traditional job description, this document supports many organizationally-based Human Resources (HR) functions. The job description is used to recruit and select employees, manage performance, identify and provide training and development opportunities, aid succession planning, gauge remuneration and reward packages, and many other aspects of Human Resource Management (HRM). This work document is supposed to be the bedrock of human activities in the organization. Our reliance on the job description puts considerable pressure on getting the structure and content of this document right.

The job description is based on the tasks employees are supposed to do in their job. Most organizations structure the job description around the specifications of the job's duties and activities; the adoption of a task-based approach. The task-based approach has its origins in "scientific management," with Frederick Taylor's notion that jobs could be studied and specified, and that work methods used for jobs could be improved and rationalized.

The first generation job description

Along with Peter Drucker, Frederick Taylor was undoubtedly one of the most influential management thinkers of all time. Over 100 years ago, his book, *Principles of Scientific Management,*[2] revolutionized the workplace. Taylor believed that we could and should quarantine jobs into a clear process so that the performance of the worker could be measured, monitored, and improved. This worked brilliantly on the Henry Ford motor car assembly line. From Taylor's scientific management philosophy, the first generation job description evolved as a natural extension. With some alterations, 100 years later we are still using the same document! But the work people do is radically different. The task-based or first generation job description is actually doing more harm than good.

Jobs are designed by managers. The role of management is essentially to define, control, standardize, and evaluate work processes and practices. One of the fundamental building blocks of organizational work is the concept of the job. Based on the principles of scientific management, the traditional job description is a mechanism of managerialism.

Historically, the job description has been the vehicle for documenting a set of relatively inflexible and tangible tasks and activities performed by a worker.

The job analysis movement of the 1940s was the catalyst for the development of the job description. Jobs were originally designed based on analyses that focused solely on the tasks that needed to be done. In the first generation job description, no real consideration was given to employee attributes to perform these tasks, at least not in a documented sense. It wasn't until the late 1960s that job analysis took into account the traits of the employee.

A job analysis method called the Position Analysis Questionnaire (PAQ) was developed that incorporated employee-oriented competencies. The PAQ signaled a significant shift away from the task-oriented approach of formulating job descriptions by putting some emphasis on the worker. The PAQ opened the door to considering the qualities, traits, and skills required by the job-holder. Job analyses progressed from here to refer to these person-centric attributes as competencies.

It is likely that this trend toward considering employee traits will continue in the foreseeable future. As organizations become flatter, and the boundaries around specific jobs less clearly defined, generating task-based job descriptions may not play a central role in the practices of HRM in the future.[3] Although many organizations have moved to a competency-based model of job analysis, the majority of job descriptions are still written in job-specific terms. Managers understandably still want to construct a periphery around each job. It is obviously difficult to change the entrenched habits of 200 years of industry. As William Bridges reminds us, jobs may be disappearing, but work still remains.[4] Defining boundaries around work responsibilities is still considered important to managers and employees alike. People want to know where they stand and what they are accountable for.

I also think the need for clearly defined and specific task responsibilities is still important. But organizational leaders – and in particular, HR professionals – have been slow to shift the emphasis in the analysis of work away from the job and towards the job-holder. But some progress has been made: Task-specific and competency-specific information is now viewed as important in describing what people do at work. Although competency models are still developing, they have some way to go to match the prominence of task-specific information in the job description documentation. But non-job roles people perform – although recognized as important – are in most cases not fully integrated into the description of work documents. The important roles people perform in the work-setting – apart from the job tasks and activities they are expected to complete – need further attention. *The End of the Job Description* intends to bring these non-job roles into sharper focus.

But let's not get ahead of ourselves. We need to understand the short-comings of the first generation job description and how this led to what I refer to as the second generation job description.

Weaknesses of the task-specific job description

Task-based job descriptions, although still prevalent today, are criticized for three broad reasons. First, there is too much concentration on a specific job and a subsequent lack of weight on the individual job-holder's ability to carry out the work. Second, with the concentration on tasks and activities, first generation job descriptions are not equipped to take into account important work that is not job-specific. And third, the task-based approach assumes that by clearly identifying the work that needs doing, putting the "right" person in that job naturally leads to productivity and performance. Balancing person-specific information with task-specific information goes some way to alleviating these deficiencies.

However, it is worth considering these shortcomings in more detail for a moment. Tasks can and do become outdated or obsolete very quickly in a fast-paced work environment. For instance, some tasks can be automated while others can be replaced or reformed. This means the shelf-life of a task-based job description is very short in a dynamic work-setting. By the time the ink has dried on a first generation job description, it can be obsolete and of little value to the job-holder, their manager, or the organization.

A job analysis based solely on tasks and activities discourages innovation and continuous improvement. The first generation job description states what has to be done and how it is to be done. Doing different tasks, or doing tasks differently, can be considered working outside the parameters of the task-specific job description. This "unconventional" activity will most likely be frowned upon by the employee's colleagues and manager who value an adherence to the letter of the job description. Accordingly, flexible deployment of skills-sets is hindered. Worse still, experimenting with new ways and means to accomplish the tasks and activities explicitly stated in the job description is suppressed, even if these new approaches and methods prove to be more productive. The first generation job description promoted stability and predictability – the opposite effect to innovation and continuous improvement.

Another drawback in the absence of competency information from the task-specific job description is the difficulty in evaluating performance in similar jobs across an organization. Apart from comparing the performance of two people doing the same sort of work, it is challenging enough to evaluate one employee's performance. Without any skills-criteria to measure against, how can one assess performance with any degree of objectivity? Simply stating the tasks of the job, with no related competencies required to conduct those tasks, the job description has no performance or organizational context.

It is quite common for the same task to be listed in two or more job descriptions. But that same task often requires an entirely different skill-level in another position. For example, consider the task of *budget preparation*. Preparing a budget for a supervisor with six team members and a set of tangible resources can be less complicated than preparing a budget for an administrative role with 100 employees and many intangible resources. Both tasks require different skill-levels despite being essentially the same activity. Being able to make valid comparisons across an organization based exclusively on the tasks employees do becomes problematic. A comparative analysis of skills is important for a host of HR practices, such as remuneration and pay scales, and performance management and measurement.

Apart from the difficulties in comparing tasks across several jobs, a task-based job analysis diminishes the usefulness of the job description for other HR practices. For instance, a first generation job description – without mention of competencies – makes it harder to confidently select the best applicant for the job, to induct them into the business, to train and develop them, and to manage their performance. All of these limitations undoubtedly lead to the inclusion of the competency dimension and what I refer to as the second generation job description.

What is a competency?

I have and will continue to use the word *competency* throughout *The End of the Job Description*, so it is important to clarify what I mean by this term. There are many different interpretations of the word competency. Charles Woodruffe offers a suitable definition from an employment perspective. He says a competency is "a set of behavior patterns that the incumbent needs to bring to a position in order to perform its tasks and functions with competence."[5] These behaviors can be derived from specialized knowledge, a particular skill, or a type of attitude.

Let me define the dimensions of knowledge, skill, and attitude as they relate to a competency.

Knowledge as it relates to a job is specialized information necessary to perform a particular task in that line-of-work. For instance, knowledge can be technical know-how needed to operate a piece of machinery. Job skills are learned techniques to perform a particular task. For example, the ability to complete a thorough risk analysis requires a particular set of skills, including being able to assess a situation or process objectively, using a set of criteria. An attitude is a state-of-mind that is *de rigueur* to successfully executing a task. For example, to be successful in selling, the salesperson needs an attitude of resilience. A resilient attitude is indispensable in combating the inevitable and relentless barrage of knockbacks and rejection. The three dimensions of a competency – knowledge, skill, and attitude – are precursors of behaviors that demonstrate whether a task or role has been done correctly.

The second generation job description

The limitations of the task-based format of the job description and the advantages of strategically aligning HR functions in the business, has prompted the inclusion of competency information. Many well-known companies and organizations, such as Boeing, Microsoft, and the United States Department of State, are already using competency models for several processes, including selection, appraisal, promotion, and training. Since the basic job description is potentially the foundation of virtually all HR functions, it is imperative that it includes a skills component.

Despite the apparent difference between task-based and skills-based formats, there is some overlap between the two dimensions. Scholars refer to this cross-over as an "inferential leap."[6] In the context of a job analysis, an inferential leap refers to the use of the task-related information in a position to identify the matching competencies to perform the job. Specifically, the *leap* is the conclusion or inference of the required knowledge, skills, and attitudes to perform the tasks cited in the job description. This competency-based or second generation job description was initially crafted by assuming the set of skills necessary to undertake the tasks.

Competency-based job descriptions are pretty much common place now. Beginning with the inferential leap, detailed and standardized competency frameworks have now been developed across all industries.

The second generation job description is a logical progression from the task-based format or first generation job description.

Strengths of the competency-based job description

This progress from first to second generation plugged some of the weaknesses in the task-based job analysis. Consequently, there are several advantages in using a competency-based approach in formulating the job description. Briefly, the advantages are summarized below:

- A competency-based approach provides criteria to make distinctions between various levels of performance.
- Competency models for job descriptions can be linked with performance, whereas task-based models have, at best, a tenuous link.
- The use of the competency-based approach in the formulation of job descriptions can add a degree of flexibility in workforce planning.
- Organizations that use competency-based approaches can take advantage of a more adaptable workforce by recruiting, selecting, and training individuals with the skills required for successful performance.

With a competency focus on employees' skills and potential, this is likely to be compelling to individuals who want to seek out opportunities to learn and grow. From the recruiter's perspective, competencies can be used to match a job with an individual during the employee selection process. And for an employee, an explicit account of the necessary skills in a job description is likely to be preferable to making the inferential leap I spoke about earlier.

With these advantages over the task-related job description, it is unsurprising that most organizations have graduated to competency-based or second generation models of the job description.

By way of example, and in the interests of clarity, a typical task-related component of a customer service role is *processing orders from customers*. Using the knowledge, skills, and attitude competency dimensions framework, this would typically include *knowledge* of all documentation and recording processes for customer orders; *skill* to complete orders accurately and in a timely fashion; and the *attitude* to process orders as a matter of priority. These dimensions clarify the expectations of the job-holder regarding the task of processing orders from customers; they change the accent from the task to the person.

The second generation job description, with its focus on competencies, is a more comprehensive document than the first generation job description. But it is still structured around a set of job tasks and not a series of roles. Some non-job roles people play at work are becoming as significant as the job tasks they are expected to perform. So, it is timely to move to a third generation; that is, a move from the job description to the role description.

A T T H E C O A L F A C E ...

From length of service to adding value

In the past, employees were rewarded for their length of service to a company. Those that stuck with the same company for a relatively long time were entitled to certain privileges. Now companies want employees who can willingly add value in their role within their work-setting, regardless of their tenure.

This means that employees who contribute in constructive ways outside the scope of their job description are potentially more valuable than those who stick stringently to the letter of their job description. However, the issue of what exactly constitutes work performance has been widely debated by management experts. It is only relatively recently that non-job behaviors have been universally considered to be critical to overall organizational performance.

Despite all this focus on performance, most performance management systems are still substandard. These systems more often than not ignore – or only pay lip service to – aspects of work performance that are not specifically job-related. The best illustration of this is the conventional building block for performance systems: the job description.

Rarely is non-job-related performance criteria mentioned in the job description. For example, value-added behaviors such as making suggestions for improvements, being a good organizational citizen, and displaying extraordinary customer service are often excluded from the job description. And if they are mentioned, it is only in vague terms. Yet it is hard to deny that these behaviors are value-added behaviors that inevitably contribute to overall organizational performance.[7]

The third generation role description

As I define it, the role description states the tasks that need doing for a job (first generation), the competencies required to do those tasks (second generation), and the non-job roles employees are expected to take on organizationally (third generation). The job description – whether it is first or second generation – fails to take into account the organizational non-job roles people have a responsibility to play as an employee. Beyond the technically proficient worker, it is the successful execution of important non-job roles that adds value to the organization and individual.

Job tasks that people perform are still critically important, and will inevitably continue to be so. But non-job roles are also critical factors in work performance. Employees, whether they realize it or not, play numerous roles in the workplace, apart from doing the tasks cited in the job description. Some of these non-job roles are performed consciously and others unconsciously. But the attention or inattention of some non-job behaviors can have a significant bearing on organizational and individual performance. *The End of the Job Description* provides HR practitioners with a rationale and methodology to convert job descriptions to role descriptions. It is role descriptions that I believe capture the totality of what is expected of employees in the new world of work.

A survey in 2005 of HR executives from 373 public and private US companies found that 100 per cent of the top 20 companies and 73 per cent of all other companies integrated competencies into their business practices.[8] This illustrates the strong commitment to a shift to the person-centered focus of the job description. The changing nature of work, its increasing complexity, and the escalating intensity from local to global competition are the drivers for progressing from the job-specific to person-specific job description. Nonetheless, this important shift in HRM practices still has some way to go, as I have discussed.

A large chunk of person-centered dimension is still largely missing from the work document. This third underdeveloped component answers the following three questions:

- What universally important non-job roles are employees expected to play as members of the organization?
- What are the key elements of these roles?
- What are the KPIs for these elements and roles?

Briefly, the third generation role description covers the employee's organization-specific role.

The End of the Job Description is about making sense of the missing organization-specific dimension of work. Integrating this dimension into the work document produces what I refer to as the third generation role description. This dimension – the organizational dimension – is inferred, inconclusive, or missing in the second generation job description. By fully assimilating this additional dimension in the documentation of work, the role description covers the job, individual, and organization dimensions of work.

Figure 1.1 illustrates the three generations of the work document; starting from the top, the top two layers are the first and second generation job description. The third generation at the bottom of the model is the role description. On the left-hand side are the three dimensions starting with the job, then the individual, and finally, the organization. On the

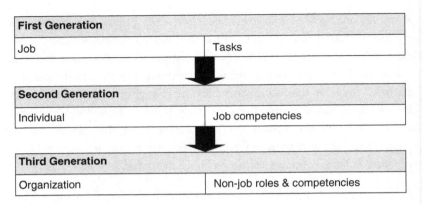

FIGURE 1.1 Evolution of the work document

right-hand side is the focus of each dimension, beginning with the tasks of the job, then progressing to the competencies associated with the job, and finally, the non-job roles and their competencies. The role description builds on the two generations and includes a third dimension.

The four core non-job roles I have included in the third generation role description model are critical for organizational performance. They form the non-job roles framework. They cover the following competencies:

- Attitude and enthusiasm.
- Ability to work in teams.
- Skills-development.
- Contributing to improvements in the workplace.

I discuss this non-job roles framework in subsequent chapters and in greater detail in Part II.

The concept of the job as we originally understood it has changed considerably since the birth of industry. With some moderate adjustments, we still design work around the old concept of a job. In the job description we have neglected – or paid too little attention to – the organizational roles employees are ever more relied upon to perform. These non-job roles are becoming more and more important in terms of individual and organizational performance. For instance, we expect people to come to work with a positive attitude and enthusiasm. We expect employees to be able to work together in permanent and temporary teams. We expect employees to continually grow and develop their skills-sets at all stages of their career. We expect employees to be involved in the continuous development of the business. Thriving enterprises in the 21st century are most likely filled with employees who exemplify these organizational competencies.

Due to these rising expectations, I believe HR professionals need to think of the work people do as a series of roles rather than as one clear-cut, specific job. This one clear-cut job concept is characteristic of Taylor's assembly line worker of the early 20th century. The challenge as I see it is to build upon the second generation job description to include non-job roles that impact work and organizational performance. Replacing the job description with the role description more aptly reflects the transformative nature of organizational work. The traditional job description, despite a move towards competency-based models, is still concentrated on a bundle of job-specific tasks. This is a hangover from Frederick Taylor's scientific management philosophy. Organizational work is now less functional and more project-driven; it is nothing like the segmented and conventional work of the Ford assembly line.

And yet we still hold on to the idea that the best way to measure, monitor, and control employees and the work they do is through a narrow frame of reference called a job description. It is timely to expand the predominantly restricted task-centric document that defines the specific requirements of a job. We should take on a more expansive model of work that goes beyond the skills, knowledge, and attitude necessary to do a particular job. Putting it concisely, we ought to describe the work that needs doing in an organizational-setting rather than defining a single job that has to be done.

In Chapter 2, we look at the concept of performance at work. As the subtitle of *The End of the Job Description* states, we must shift from a job-focus to a performance-focus.

The **Top 10** Key Points …

1. Work is now more multifaceted, the boundaries around the responsibilities of employees are ambiguous, and indicators of performance are different.

2. The job description is used to recruit and select employees, manage performance, identify and provide training and development opportunities, aid succession planning, gauge remuneration and reward packages, and many other aspects of HRM.

3. The job description is based on the tasks employees are expected to do in their job. This is the first generation version of the job description.

4. The job analysis movement of the 1940s was the catalyst for the development of the job description. Jobs were originally designed based on analyses that focused solely on the tasks that needed to be done.

5. A competency can be defined as "a set of behavior patterns that the incumbent needs to bring to a position in order to perform its tasks and functions with competence."

6. The limitations of the task-based format of the job description and the advantages of strategically aligning HR functions in the business, has prompted the inclusion of competency information.

7. The second generation job description is a logical progression from the task-based format or first generation job description.

8. Integrating the organization-specific dimension into the work document produces what is referred to as the third generation role description.

9. The non-job roles framework in the third generation role description covers the following attributes: attitude and enthusiasm, ability to work in teams, skills-development, and contributing to improvements in the workplace.

10. HR professionals need to think of the work people do as a series of roles rather than as a clear-cut, specific job characteristic of Taylor's assembly line worker of the early 20th century.

chapter 2

The Harmful Impact of the Job Description on HRM

The pitfalls in the HRM practices ... resulting from an over-reliance of the job description can be overcome by replacing this outdated work document with a role description. A role description captures both the job and non-job roles employees are expected to play in the workplace.

Maryanne, a new customer service officer was being inducted and trained by Felicity, a long-time member of a customer service team. The new employee appreciated her trainer's experience and knowledge and quickly gained a level of confidence in her new job. One thing she also quickly learned was that a key performance measure in her new job description was how quickly visitors were processed, not how well their inquiries were handled.

"It feels like churn and burn," Maryanne told her trainer. "Lots of these people are coming back again and again with the same issue and they're upset at us for not giving them the right information. It seems like we should be spending more time finding out what the real issue is when they first come in."

"Not our problem," said Felicity in response to Maryanne's protest. "That's the manager's problem. They just don't want to see lines of people."

"Besides, it doesn't say anything about spending more time than necessary in your job description, does it?" "Go with what's in your job description and you can't go wrong, Maryanne," advised the trainer.

Although Maryanne wasn't content with this response, as a new employee, she persevered with things until she took complete ownership of the job and then started engaging in richer conversations with customers to more effectively solve their issues. Maryanne also rationalized that by doing so, she would minimize repeat visits and provide better customer service.

"You're taking too long with the customers," she was told by Royce, her manager, after a month on the job. Explaining her rationale and commitment to delivering a better service was to no avail.

"That's not your concern," she was told by Royce.[1]

Excelling at a job and performing at work are not necessarily the same thing. Plenty of people are doing what is required of them based on their job description, but failing to perform. Put another way, you can be meticulously doing a particular job, covering all the KRAs in the job description, and still underperform. It can work in reverse too; you can be performing brilliantly without necessarily following the exact requirements specified in the job description. As we discussed in Chapter 1, the second generation job description describes the task requirements of a job and the competencies necessary for their successful accomplishment. But performing in an organizational context is more than completing the tasks cited in the job description.

For instance, possessing a negative attitude can adversely affect performance. A person being constantly critical and chronically unenthusiastic will most likely negatively impact the performance of those they work with closely, not to mention themselves. Although most of us accept that attitude affects performance, the right attitude one ought to bring to the workplace is not usually stated in the job description. And on the rare occasion that attitude is mentioned in the document, it is expressed in vague terms. Attitude and enthusiasm constitute one of four organizational roles in the non-job roles framework and these are not generally covered in the task-specific job description. Nonetheless, attitude – as we know – has a significant influence on organizational performance.

Here is another example: What if someone is technically skilled in their job, but is a pain in the backside to deal with? What if they aren't a team player, refusing to work collaboratively with their colleagues? An inability to work in a team is going to be detrimental to performance, isn't it? An employee's superior technical competency may not make up for self-centered or selfish behavior. The competency of working with and through other people constructively is not always cited in the job description, or if it is, it gets a brief mention towards the end of the document. Again, this key non-job competency affects performance. A third example is an employee in an administrative position refusing to learn a new computer software system. This employee stubbornly decides to continue to do a time-consuming task with an outdated program, even when the new software program takes a fraction of the time. This reluctance to learn a new skill has harmful performance consequences. The stubbornness of refusing to learn something new is slowing down operations. You and I know people like this; they won't openly embrace new learning opportunities. But know the harmful cost this has on productivity. Being in a continual state of learning and displaying a willingness to grow personally and technically is an asset in a VUCA environment, as we covered in Chapter 1. The job description again either makes a fleeting statement about "a preparedness to learn on the job," or says nothing at all about the non-job competency of career development.

And finally, what about the person who consistently adopts the attitude that "if it isn't broke, don't fix it" or "this is the way we have always done things around here"? You and I hear these kinds of statements from time-to-time in our workplaces, don't we? Offering constructive suggestions – or at least being willing to try new approaches at work – is an important non-job competency linked to organizational performance. How can we do things faster, with less effort, in less time, with less cost, with more effect, with greater impact, in safer ways? These are important questions to be considered. Although it sounds a simple premise, we are all waiting despairingly for Peter Senge's *learning organization* to materialize, some 25 years since he wrote about it! Creating a learning organization is a complex matter beyond the scope of my book. Nonetheless, its complexity shouldn't discourage us from expecting employees to consider ways and means of improving the organization they work in. Alternatively, someone refusing to adopt a new approach sabotages others for wanting to try a new approach; or unwillingness to change their old ways and habits is stifling progress and harmful to productivity. An openness to offer or try new methods at work is a critically important non-job competency, and not an unreasonable expectation of an employee. But if continuous improvement and innovation is stated in the job description, it's typically expressed like this: *The job-holder needs to demonstrate a willingness to be flexible and innovative.* It's a vague and familiar statement that has little meaning. And due to its ambiguity, when challenged, an employee can simply dismiss their lack of commitment to continuous improvement by stating something along the lines of, "I didn't think that statement in the job description related to this situation." Or, if there is no reference to this non-job competency in the job description, the employee can say with justification, "Being innovative is not stated on my job description." Either way, the employee is off the hook.

Briefly, these are four illustrations to demonstrate the relationship between non-job roles and performance. The incompleteness of the job description by not covering these non-job roles adequately, or at all, has harmful performance implications for all HRM practices in an organization. Figure 2.1 illustrates the core HRM practices that are shaped by the job description.

I will discuss each of these six usual HRM practices in Figure 2.1 and how the task-specific job description has a harmful impact on the practices. Although these practices are integrated, I will discuss each separately in the interests of clarity.

I made the claim in Chapter 1 that the job description is doing more harm than good in the workplace of the 21st century. In this chapter I want to back up that assertion.

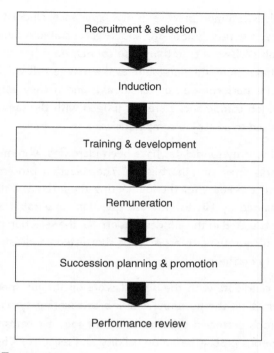

FIGURE 2.1 / **HRM practices**

/ **Recruitment and selection**

Unless the employee is recruited internally, the first contact HR has with a new employee is during the selection process, typically in an interview. The conventional practice of selecting the suitable candidate based upon the job-related criteria in the job description can backfire with disastrous consequences. Nonetheless, there is pretty much universal acceptance that the best criteria for recruiting and selecting employees are job competencies. On the surface, this seems perfectly valid, fair, and reliable; it appears to be a very sensible and rational process to find the right person to fill a job vacancy. But what doesn't make sense is the exclusive reliance on the job's task-related competencies to select a new employee.

However, this is common practice in my experience. Under the guise of "best practice," we usually look for and select a suitable candidate with the "right" job skills-set fit; nothing else counts; no other criteria comes into play. What's more, the non-job roles the new recruit will inescapably perform or not perform are not considered; and if they are taken into account, non-job competencies are not judged with the same thoroughness as that used to assess job competencies.

Once several worthy candidates have been identified who meet the job-specific criteria, they are "short-listed." The selection process begins to find the "best" candidate for the job. During the interview, the selection panel is reminded by HR to only ask questions applicable to the task-related aspects stated in the job description. So, the selection panel develops a series of questions to assess each shortlisted candidate's technical competency to do the job.

Usually, the candidate with the highest score on the job-specific criteria gets an offer to fill the position. A task-based scoring system evaluates each candidate's perceived capacity to do the job; it creates the perception of a rigorous process based on validity and reliability. The candidate judged to have the greatest mastery of the job tasks gets the nod.

Attitude and enthusiasm, the ability to work constructively with a variety of colleagues and stakeholders, the candidate's readiness to develop personally and technically, and their preparedness to question the *status quo*, are bypassed in the quest to find the most technically-proficient candidate. Sometimes, these non-job competencies are taken into account; but if they are taken into consideration, they are of secondary importance to their technical competency.

Yet ironically, the selection panel is very aware of the value and importance of these non-job competencies and their weight on organizational performance. The selection panel typically makes some assumptions about the candidate's ability to fulfill these non-job roles. But by-and-large, they are compelled to "stick to the script"; that is, the focus is on the technical qualifications and job skills. The bottom-line is this: We select an employee predominantly on task specifications embedded in the job description.

In the interests of maintaining reliability in the selection process, a member of the selection panel asks the same set of questions to the referees of the successful candidate. Again, by doing so, it reinforces the job functions as the premier (and only, in most cases) selection criteria; and the candidate that best meets this criteria, gets the job. This practice diminishes the status of non-job roles in the selection process, even though we know they still count in work performance! Disturbingly, it is only by accident, assumption, or gut feel that the selection panel pays attention to a candidate's non-job competencies. Worst of all, it is later, after several weeks or months on the job, that it becomes apparent the willingness and ability of the new employee to contribute beyond their job obligations. This is too late.

To illustrate the point, after the probationary period lapsed, Lisa – one of the selection panelists – turns to Rod, another on the panel and says, with a rueful expression, "If only we had known that Bill (the new employee) would treat everyone with contempt and disrespect when we interviewed him several months ago." "If only!" repeats Rod with a sigh.

Non-job competencies are not assessed thoroughly, if at all, during the selection process. Yet they have a major bearing on performance. By evaluating the worth of a candidate solely on the limits of the job specifications, we aren't taking into account an all-encompassing interpretation of work performance. Sadly, the lens we use for recruitment and selection is based on the job description and little else.

Induction

Once the selection ritual is over, the new employee commences their new job. Most new employees, particularly those recruited from outside the organization, are understandably a mix of excitement and apprehension on day one. At the same time, the starting employee is eager to learn and receptive to new information and the environment they are exposed to. This early stage of the employment cycle is a golden opportunity to positively shape and mold a set of productive habits at work, or at least break old, unhelpful habits in a new employee. We understand the importance and value of a well-run induction program for new recruits.

A thorough induction program includes a mix of information and exposure. The program predominantly includes information relevant to completing the requirements of the job, the company, and its policies and processes, such as health and safety policies, and matters pertinent to the team or department the employee is part of. During this onboarding process, there is a strong emphasis on preparing the new employee to undertake their job role. There is less emphasis placed on preparing the employee for their organizational role. This orientation further entrenches the partiality in the selection process on job tasks. From the early stages in the induction process, the new employee can be forgiven for thinking that non-job roles and their competencies are comparatively insignificant to their employment success. On the contrary, a good supervisor sits down with a new team member during the first few weeks of employment and discusses their non-job role. Further, the leader who is mindful articulates their expectations of the new employee in their organizational role, apart from their job role. But alas, as we know, good leaders are in short supply.

In most cases, the new employee's supervisor was involved in their selection; and that process – in all probability – focused exclusively on job-related competencies. But good leadership practice, as I mentioned, is to redress this bias. In the early stages of settling into a new job, the leader ought to discuss the new recruit's role and responsibility as an organizational citizen. We need to remind ourselves that an employee is going to be most impressionable in the early stage in a new job. Although potentially receptive to the leader's standards, the new recruit has their own expectations of their organizational role too. Sometimes, the views of the leader and new employee may not be the same; that is, the new job-holder's expectations may not be in sync with their boss's outlook. The induction process is a great opportunity to discuss these different perspectives; to have a conversation about performance that goes beyond the KRAs listed in the new employee's job description.

But unfortunately this occasion in the beginning stages of employment is not often utilized by leaders to discuss and agree upon non-job expectations. Instead, the early interactions between the boss and new recruit are typically going to involve on-the-job activities. This early task-specific interaction further reinforces the impression that the non-job roles people play at work are of less relevance and importance.

Training and development

As the employee passes the probationary period, they are exposed to training and development opportunities. Most of these learning opportunities are technical training programs designed to improve their current and future job competencies. Training programs that build non-job competencies, such as team development, are more prevalent than they once were, but less prominent than job competency development.

Technical training designed to improve job-specific competencies has been the conventional approach to employee development since the birth of industry. Training with this technical orientation helps employees develop their skills-set to do their job with more capability. Although technical training is unquestionably essential, companies and employees need more than technical skills and know-how to survive and prosper in the rapidly changing marketplace. Employees across all industries are facing – on a daily basis – problems, challenges, and dilemmas that can't necessarily be solved using procedural knowledge and skills learnt from a technical training course. There is not always a convenient, clearly defined process to resolve the increasing array of complex problems employees are bombarded with. The answers to these "wicked" problems are not always found in the company manual or in the technical training curriculum.

Managers, who understand this, take an eclectic view of people development that includes both technical and non-technical training and development interventions. In practice, this means sponsoring both technical and non-technical learning opportunities. By adopting this assorted approach to Human Resource Development (HRD), managers are investing in the whole person, not just in the employee's functional capacities. But because the job description is heavily geared towards job-related tasks, it is somewhat harder to justify spending money in the non-technical domain.

Training that directly assists an employee to learn a new, or improve an existing, job-related competency, can be referred to as the *production-centered* approach to learning. There are two other dimensions of learning: the *person-centered* and *problem-centered* approaches. These two approaches, while increasingly being recognized as relevant to performance-enhancement, are significantly less popular than the production-centered approach. The concentration on the task-related aspects in the job description means the production-centered approach takes precedence most of the time.

However, hyper-competition and the rapidly changing and unpredictable marketplace has elevated the importance of being able to solve unique and challenging problems and displaying initiative, sometimes on the spur of the moment. This environment can be summed up with the popular acronym, VUCA. VUCA stands for *volatility, uncertainty, complexity,* and *ambiguity*; characteristics of the modern world we live in, and are all familiar with.[2]

Competencies to deal with the VUCA environment are outside the realm of the job description. To be flexible and enterprising are now core competencies for all employees, regardless of the technical sophistication of their job. Today's workplace needs a wide-ranging perspective on training and development beyond a reliance on technical training. This brings into sharper focus the person-centered and problem-centered approach to learning.

To be flexible and enterprising are now core competencies for all employees, regardless of the technical sophistication of their job.

Let's look a bit closer at the three predominant philosophical training and development perspectives. You'll find a more comprehensive account in one of my other books, *The End of the Performance Review*.[3]

Production-centered approach

The conventional training and development method emphasizing a job-centric perspective is the production-centered approach. A production-centered approach stresses the job dimension of performance. The rationale for this method is the direct transfer of learning; that is, the tangible link between training and improved job skills. Improving employees' current job skills enhances productivity on the job. Of the three approaches to training, the production-centered approach is the one directly related to the specifics of the job description.

For example, training programs that develop employees' mastery of the use of machines, technology, or processes that are job-specific, are production-centered. Production-centered learning is likely to have a direct job productivity payoff. In other words, there is a more tangible return on investment for boosting an employee's efficiency and effectiveness in performing their day-to-day job function. Success of the production-centered approach is measured by an employee becoming more technically proficient.

Person-centered approach

A second philosophical perspective on learning is the person-centered approach. This approach emphasizes personal development. Person-centered learning has an indirect link between the learning experience and work performance. The primary motive for investing in an employee's personal development is the enhancement of personal qualities that impact positively on their overall work performance. Unlike the production-centered approach, the person-centered approach has a more tenuous link to performance. This philosophy of learning is based on the idea that capable people make capable employees in a variety of contexts.

For example, training programs that improve people's mastery of themselves – such as courses on goal setting, personal motivation, time management, and emotional intelligence – can have a resultant payoff in terms of increased productivity. The incentive for sponsoring personal development programs is based on the premise that by developing people – the organization's most precious resource – it may lead to them being more proficient in their current and future work practices. Over the last quarter of a century, the growing popularity of the person-centered approach suggests this idea has some foundation.

Person-centered approach in action

The Sir Edmund Hillary Outdoor Pursuits Centre of New Zealand was founded in 1972. The late Sir Edmund Hillary was a patron of the center. The vision of the center is to provide people with the opportunity to take part in adventurous outdoor activities. People who take part in such adrenalin-producing activities tend to experience intrinsic changes. Positive gains are made in self-esteem, skills are developed, and social interactions are enhanced. Competition is subdued while cooperation is encouraged. A number of successful corporations have put staff and managers through outdoor programs such as those offered by the center. Through these experiences, participants explore values and recognize weaknesses in themselves, and have the potential to create positive changes in themselves and their organizations.[4]

Problem-centered approach

The third school of learning is referred to as the problem-centered approach. The focus of this approach is on improving employees' ability to solve problems. This betters an employee's capacity to make more effective decisions on the job. The rationale for this approach is the connection between problem-solving competence and organizational performance. In other words, the primary motive for investing in problem-centered learning is to improve the employee's decision-making aptitude, so they can better deal with unpredictable challenges they face in their job.

This training and development approach is based on the idea that employees will make better decisions at work if they have the necessary knowledge, skills, and attitude to analyze and respond to random problems. As a consequence of this type of training, the employee is more likely to exercise autonomy when dealing with ambiguous challenges affecting their work. This means the employee is less dependent on their supervisor.

For example, topics such as creative problem-solving techniques, research skills, or analysis of typical workplace case studies can develop problem-solving capabilities.

AT THE COAL FACE ...

Problem-centered approach in action

Julie, Executive Manager of Learning and Development for a large, well-known bank, was charged with responsibility for revamping the bank's approach to inducting customer service representatives (CSRs) in retail banking services. After looking at the turnover rates and gathering information from the five conversations,[5] she decided it was time to act.

From what she had heard in these conversations, the bank had a challenge to reduce the high rates of turnover in CSRs in the first 12 weeks of their employment. Employees had told their managers in these conversations that they lacked confidence in their skills and knowledge. The approach in the induction program was the place to start, she concluded.

From a learning perspective, the new approach enabled participants to better analyze situations and source information more effectively. This policy, supported by a continuous coaching component, involved a partnership between the participant, their branch manager, and a "buddy," who was an experienced CSR. With this support, participants were required to take ownership of their learning and complete a series of tasks. In addition to this, they would work with their branch manager to identify strengths and areas of improvement through daily check-ins, debriefs, and feedback sessions.

> Collaborative learning occurs through the use of problem-based learning, simulations, and research. During off-the-job learning periods, participants would work in learning sets or groups to explore customer situations they would encounter in real life. They were encouraged to analyze the situation, explore how they would respond to it, and complete any customer transactions using simulations or "role play."
>
> To date, the CSR induction program was able to deliver an 8 per cent reduction in voluntary turnover in the first six months.[6]

In summary, there is a clear preference for production-centered learning in industry. The vast majority of this training is directly related to learning and developing the technical aspects of the job cited in the job description. But a multi-dimensional strategy, pulling all three training and development threads together, is a better strategy. In practice, I'd suggest one third of the training and development budget be assigned to each of the three approaches. This will rapidly redress the imbalance towards the production-centered approach borne out of the task-centric job description.

Remuneration

Assessing the pay levels of employees is never an easy task. When it comes to evaluating pay rises, we again tend to rely on the strict letter of the job description to inform our decision. This is done under the guise of "fairness" and "impartiality." It's considered too risky to stray beyond the confines of the six to eight KRAs in the job description to make judgments about whether to give an employee a pay rise or not. To judge other factors apart from the job description is thought to be too subjective.

Our image of ourselves as objective decision-makers is misguided. As human beings, we are prone – far more than we would like to believe – to being biased and subjective in virtually everything we decide upon. It is impossible to be completely objective people at work. Yet this is what we endeavor to do; to be objective. We deceive ourselves that we make rational and logical decisions, particularly in the workplace; it is a fallacy.

Due to this erroneous belief that managers are objective decision-makers, they don't take into account non-job competencies in remuneration considerations. Non-job competencies are viewed as a peripheral matter in the assessment of pay levels. More specifically, non-job competencies – such as one's attitude and enthusiasm, ability to work in a team, readiness to develop oneself, and contributing to the efficiency and effectiveness of the workplace – are not naturally taken into account; they don't factor in remuneration decisions. Further, managers are disinclined to raise any of these non-job roles during the remuneration interview. The manager doesn't want to "muddy the waters" by raising issues not directly related to the task-based KPIs in the job description. The employee on the receiving end of the remuneration interview knows that these non-job roles won't be factored into the assessment of remuneration levels, at least not openly. So the employee is also reluctant to raise any substantial non-job contribution as a supporting argument for a pay rise.

But the reality is substantially different. Employees performing or not performing in any of these organizational roles I have mentioned impact performance, either positively or negatively. Just because contributions (or lack of contributions) in the non-job dimension can't be measured by a number, doesn't mean they are any less significant contributors to performance. For instance, an employee positively exercising their non-job roles can do, among many other things, the following:

- Elevate morale and improve organizational climate.
- Build teamwork.
- Create harmonious relationships.
- Upgrade systems and processes.
- Apply new skills for the benefit and betterment of the work unit.
- Increase the performance of their work unit.

Notwithstanding these obvious benefits, in the interests of being seen to be objective and impartial, the pay rise decision boils down to an evaluation of the task-specific KPIs in the job description.

Succession planning and promotion

Succession planning is the practice of identifying and developing people in the enterprise with the potential to fill key business leadership positions in the future. As with the other five HRM practices, the job description has an unhealthy sway on succession planning decisions. The decision of who replaces whom in the event of an incumbent vacating that position is nearly always made on the grounds of technical competency. Again, non-job competencies are not factored into these succession or promotion decisions as much as they ought to be. Succession planning boils down to finding or grooming an employee who has the same or similar job skills-set. It is often the case that this replacement, selected to succeed the incumbent, is from the same functional area and usually the next level down in the organizational hierarchy. This process for finding a successor is understandable. But this identification process doesn't always take into account the totality of the role.

The analysis of the successor's skill gaps is based almost exclusively on the technical perspective of the position. Although perhaps a useful starting point for succession planning, the non-job dimension of the position is frequently overlooked, or at best, given minor attention. This technical focus means the training and development plan for succession will be predominantly production-centered in orientation. Learning and development opportunities outside the scope of the job description are given lesser priority. This can be problematic.

For instance, the successive position may require extensive informal contact with many internal and external stakeholders; although this may not be explicitly stated in the job description. Someone occupying an internal service position, for example, such as a financial administration officer, needs to liaise with many people about a variety of situations and matters. For a position of this nature, being able to work with and through an extensive array of people is an important non-technical competency. However, it may not necessarily be covered in the job description. A critical non-technical competency like this can easily be overlooked, with the main attention on the technical aspects of the succession plan.

Succession planning for leadership positions, in particular, is done poorly. Going from a technical position to a leadership role requires a fundamentally different skills-set; in fact, the two skills-sets are polar opposites. For starters, the technical role is task-related and the leadership role is people-related. The technical position is about doing the work, which requires a certain technical mastery. On the other hand, the leadership position is about getting the technical job done with and through other people. The necessary skills-set for the leader is to motivate, communicate, influence, delegate, and coordinate, and so on. But all industries promote people to managerial positions on the basis of their technical know-how. The overreliance on task-specific information in the job description is the single biggest reason for this entrenched practice. Why do we continue to promote people to leadership roles on the basis of technical qualifications and skills? It is nonsensical.

For instance, just because someone is a great engineer doesn't necessarily mean they will be a great leader of engineers. In reality, the two skills-sets are not transferrable. The role of leader is beyond the technical scope of engineering. A manager's knowledge of the intimate details of the technical tasks – although useful – is less relevant than the ability to lead people to do the task. The all too familiar practice of promoting skilled technicians to managerial roles is another argument for replacing the job description with a role description.

Even the employment of a person recruited, selected, and promoted from outside the organization to a managerial position – as we have covered – is based primarily on the technical requirements of the job. The first instinct is to find out if the candidate has the technical knowledge and skills, even when the position is predominantly one based on management and leadership. And if an external applicant for a management position ticks all the technical boxes, we then assume they then have what it takes to lead others in that discipline. The job description hampers the succession planning process by limiting the scope of analysis to job competencies.

Performance review

Managers during the standard annual or biannual performance review confine their appraisals to the technical aspects of the employee's work. The manager's interest is usually whether or not the job-holder has carried out the literal requirement of the job description. This technical approach to appraising performance is generally promoted by HR. Again, the cost of sticking stringently to the letter of the job description is that vital aspects of organizational performance get by-passed or, sometimes, referred to transiently. Countless employees across all industries – even though they don't deserve it – get fair, or even good, evaluation ratings at performance review time. This is often attributable to a lack of attention paid to significant non-job roles. Many "average" or "above average" employees demonstrate substandard, or even appalling, non-job behavior.

For instance, the difficult person that everyone dislikes and refuses to associate with can, on the basis of assessing only their technical competence, pass their appraisal with flying colors. As another illustration, the person who has stopped growing and learning and therefore refuses to up-skill, multi-skill, or develop any skill, can get a satisfactory appraisal from their manager, ignoring this deficiency. These negative non-job performance traits are overlooked and so poor behavior is tacitly reinforced at appraisal time. What's more, there is no compulsion or incentive for the wayward employee to change their inappropriate and non-productive behavior. The result of these circumstances can be disastrous; the organization suffers, the employee's colleagues, their manager, and the employee themselves can suffer too.

Performing at work goes well beyond the piece of paper we refer to as job description. I have attempted to illustrate in this chapter how critically important this document is; it is the backbone for most HRM practices, six of which I've discussed here. And because of its pervasive presence, the job description severely distorts the non-job dimension of work to insignificance.

In summary, at the heart of the job description are several KRAs, representing the framework for the successful execution of a job. The employee is recruited and selected on the basis of these KRAs. They are inducted into the organization with these job-related task requirements top of mind. The employee is then trained and developed to excel in these job tasks. Further on, succession plans and promotion opportunities for the employee are based on technical nous. Further, the technically competent employee is promoted to leadership positions. Pay decisions are substantiated almost exclusively on the task-related components in the job description. We formally assess the employee's performance once or twice a year against these technical KRAs and their associated KPIs. And it's worth mentioning that we use the job description to justify sacking someone; it provides legal clout to the manager in these unfortunate circumstances. Although managers use the job description as rationalization for termination of someone's employment, it is, ironically, dreadful non-job behavior that's the real reason for dismissal. There is no doubting the omnipresent influence of the job description; it guides and informs every aspect of the employment cycle, ranging from onboarding to termination.

The pitfalls in the HRM practices we have covered in this chapter – resulting from an overreliance of the job description – can be overcome by replacing this outdated work document with a role description. The role description captures both job and non-job roles of employees; it is multi-dimensional; it doesn't focus exclusively on the task-specific job requirements. Transitioning from a job to role description, we acknowledge explicitly the totality of the employee's organizational contribution. Successfully executing a bundle of tasks we call a job will continue to be important. But the employee should bring more than their technical competence to their employment. Taking on multi-dimensional roles covering tasks and job and non-job competencies is a more realistic reflection of work performance in the 21st century. This is the essence of shifting from a job-focus to a performance-focus.

In Chapter 3, we look at the job description and its part in reinforcing the traditional working relationship between employer and employee.

The **Top 10** Key Points …

1. The incompleteness of the job description in not covering non-job roles has harmful performance implications for all HRM practices.

2. Typically, the candidate with the highest score on the job-specific criteria gets the initial offer to fill a vacancy. The task-based score evaluates the candidate's perceived capacity to do the job. Attitude and enthusiasm, the ability to work constructively with a variety of colleagues and stakeholders, the candidate's readiness to develop personally and technically, and their preparedness to question the *status quo* are not tested.

3. During the induction process, there is a strong bias in preparing the new employee to undertake their job role. There is less emphasis placed on their organizational role.

4. The vast majority of learning and development opportunities are in technical training, designed to improve their current or future job competency. Training and development programs to enhance competencies related to non-job roles are on the increase, but still limited.

5. The traditional training and development method, emphasizing a job-centric perspective, is the production-centered approach.

6. A second philosophical perspective on learning is the person-centered approach. This approach emphasizes personal development.

7. The third school of learning is referred to as the problem-centered approach. The focus of this approach is on improving employees' ability to solve problems.

8 When it comes to evaluating pay rises, we again tend to rely on the strict letter of the job description to inform our decision. This is done under the guise of "fairness and impartiality."

9 The job description hampers an organization's capacity to undertake a comprehensive succession planning process and to assist in successfully selecting suitable employees for leadership positions.

10 Managers at the conventional annual or biannual performance review confine their appraisals to the technical aspects of the job.

chapter 3

The Job Description and the Old Contract

The job description facilitates the divisions between employee and manager. What's more, a traditional thinking manager or employee, who believes in the them and us psychological contract, will focus exclusively on the job description for guidance and clarification.

Jeanette is an HR manager with a traditional approach to HRD. She refers to staffing matters as human resource matters; her training budget is almost entirely spent on production-centered or technical training. She wants employees to learn, follow, and be accountable for sticking to the literal requirements of the job description. In fact, she judges her success by how compliant people are in following organizational systems and processes. When a dilemma arises, she wants them to refer to the comprehensive manual she calls "The Bible," and to follow internal policies and procedures without deviation.

Jeanette is proud of being described as a transactional leader. Her "paperwork" is impeccably completed and she believes in observance and risk aversion. She is hands-on and has a reputation for burying herself in the detail of an issue. She wants and seeks out all the facts. Jeanette does not ask many questions but prides herself on being able to answer questions and giving the "right" answer.

Training is usually done formally in a classroom with a trainer referring to a set training manual. Good training, in her mind, is following and getting through the training workbook before the end of the time allotted. Managers in her opinion are there to lead and make decisions.

Craig replaced her as HR manager and has an entirely different learning and development philosophy. He changed the name of the department to "People, Performance and Well-being." Craig changed the training agenda and introduced such courses as lateral thinking and problem-solving; he put more emphasis on personal development.

In Craig's mind, the main thrust of his role is concerned with transforming the culture of the organization, and putting in place a plan to become an employer of choice. He left operational matters to line managers, who Craig thought were in the best position to deal with day-to-day issues. Much to the frustration of training consultants who had a good working relationship with Craig's predecessor, they were asked by Craig to shorten their sessions and break the program into smaller chunks. The trainers were used to coming in and running one-day programs and disappearing off into the sunset afterwards. He spent his first few weeks talking to employees who were at the coal face. Craig wanted to understand the challenges they faced in their jobs.[1]

For 200 years we have conceptualized the *job* as a clearly defined set of interrelated tasks. The job-holder's duty is to carry out these tasks capably in exchange for remuneration and other benefits from the employer. This agreement has been the customary psychological contract between employer and employee since the Industrial Revolution. If the employee fails to do the tasks as specified in the job description, or the employer fails to sufficiently pay the employee, the contract is breached.

The first and second generation job description is crafted to spell out the job-holder's obligations. Furthermore, the document is designed to form a common understanding of the responsibilities of the job between the job-holder and manager. The specifications are used to evaluate the job performance of the employee, and support other HR practices we covered in the last chapter. Failure to fulfill these tasks (to a documented standard) means the employee has violated the agreement in the employment relationship.

The traditional psychological contract – in which the job description has played a critical role – has been unraveling since the mid-1980s, for a variety of reasons I won't go into here. You can find more about these drivers in my book, *The 8 Values of Highly Productive Companies*.[2] Nevertheless, the way we document the work that needs doing in organizations hasn't kept pace with the evolving psychological contract; moreover, the job description has held back the development of the employment relationship.

To fully understand the role of the job description in sustaining the old contract and hindering the progression to the new contract, we need to comprehend the changing psychological contract and its impact on the world of work. By considering the changing employment relationship, we can then appreciate the futility of continuing down the same road and more fully comprehend the reason for abandoning the job description in favor of the role description.

So what exactly is a psychological contract?

Psychological contract

The psychological contract is basically a set of unwritten expectations between employees and managers. Historically, employees have had a reasonably fixed set of beliefs about the role of the employer and – by extension – management. Similarly, managers have certain generalized expectations of the job that employees are supposed to do. The old employment relationship is based on a set of clear-cut beliefs from both entities about the job the other entity should be doing to maintain their working relationship. You will find a more detailed explanation of the psychological contract or employment relationship in my book, *Attracting and Retaining Talent: Becoming an Employer of Choice*.[3]

Employees, for example, generally have an expectation that they will be paid on time, treated with respect, and given a fair go by their managers. If – in the view of one or more employees with these fundamental expectations – management doesn't uphold these ideas, then in the mind of those employees, the conventional psychological contract has been breached. In other words, management has failed to live up to their side of the unwritten agreement and consequently infringed the contract.

From the manager's point-of-view, with a customary belief about employees, they expect them to work hard, cause few problems, and arrive and leave work punctually. Once again, if an employee's behavior is inconsistent with these expectations, they have broken the contract from the manager's point-of-view. These beliefs have been handed down from generation to generation, with little real substantial change. Where do most managers learn their management skills? From their managers. And who manages the managers? Those who were previously in those managers' roles.

Conflicting psychological contracts

Despite these longstanding expectations between employee and employer, since the 1980s, the traditional psychological contract has been changing substantially, as I mentioned. Generally speaking, younger employees have vastly different expectations of work and employers than previous generations of employees. As an illustration, today's employee characteristically believes that they will be actively involved in making meaningful decisions at work. However, an older employee can have a different set of beliefs that revolve around things such as being given clear work instructions and having no real expectation of being involved in the decision-making processes of work. We shouldn't fall into the trap of categorizing these beliefs as those of *Gen Y* and *Gen X* employees on the one hand, or *Baby Boomers* on the other hand. It is true that many of the Baby Boom generation have shifted their beliefs and expectations over the years in response to cultural change, education, and their own life circumstances. And we can't generalize and say all younger employees want to be involved in decision-making.

Anyhow, with these shifting expectations that employees and employers have of one another, the first and second generation job description is no longer a viable way to document the work we do.

Apart from the changing expectations of employees, the beliefs managers have of employees have changed too. For instance, most managers now expect employees will demonstrate appropriate initiative when a situation warrants it. But pre-1980s, the majority of managers held diametrically opposite views; the belief was that employees would willingly follow instructions and be totally compliant. Today's workplace is full of these changed and conflicting sets of beliefs and expectations about the role of labor and management.

This lack of clarity and confusion of the role of both entities in the working relationships is arising as a new psychological contract emerges. The mounting ambiguity and misunderstandings are leading to more frequent communication breakdowns and mistrust between managers and employees. As I will explain in some detail, the task-specific focus of the job description is not only an impediment in clarifying these misinterpretations, it perpetuates this confusion.

Notwithstanding ambiguity, the greatest barrier to cultivating a suitable workplace culture for the VUCA environment mentioned in the previous chapter is the old psychological contract. This old contract is characterized as a "them and us" relationship between management and labor. Despite the rhetoric in the popular management books, this "them and us" culture is still pretty much alive and well in most organizations. With a disproportionate power relationship favoring the manager over an employee, the majority of interaction between the two is predominantly perfunctory and task-specific.

The job description facilitates the divisions between employee and manager. What's more, a traditional thinking manager or employee, who believes in the "them and us" psychological contract, will focus exclusively on the job description for guidance and clarification.

The four non-job roles framework and the old psychological contract don't mix. For the time-honored manager, the prevailing focus is managing employees to get the job tasks done to an acceptable standard. There is no time, or inclination, to consider non-job roles. And from the traditional-thinking employee's perspective, sticking exclusive to the duties of the job description is their priority. This limited focus on the job description from the manager and employee discounts non-job roles.

From the conservative-thinking employee's point-of-view, they are unlikely to put much energy into roles beyond the job description. For instance, roles such as displaying a positive approach to work; going out of their way to be cooperative with others; developing and bettering themselves; and making suggestions for improving the functioning of the workplace are secondary considerations. Furthermore, the employee who has been conditioned into a "them and us" psychological contract will probably think these non-job roles are not their responsibility. And in the probable occurrence that these non-job roles are absent from their job description, it strengthens the idea that they are not accountable for performing these non-job roles.

Briefly, managers who believe in the "command and control" management philosophy, are not going to see value in giving employees a more expansive set of roles beyond the scope of the tasks in the job description. And employees with a similar set of beliefs will probably view non-job roles the same way; they both think it is not the employee's duty to venture outside the bounds of the KRAs listed in their job description.

This outdated notion of the employment relationship is a significant roadblock in an organizational culture that values non-job performance. If there is no incentive to do so, the employee will shirk their so-called organizational role. The consequences are that in response to the external VUCA environment, the organization's need to be agile, flexible, and maneuverable is thwarted. The job description is the scaffolding holding in place the "them and us" psychological contract.

The job description is the scaffolding holding in place the "them and us" psychological contract.

The conflicting psychological contracts

Travis is a manager who has beliefs consistent with a new psychological contract. He believes employees have multiple organizational roles to perform and not just confined to the bundle of tasks in the job description. Travis is open to the idea of working with his employees in a collaborative working relationship. His leadership style consequently is based on dialogue with his team when the situation calls for it. Travis expects his employees to come up with suggestions for improving the flow of work, to work together as a team, to strive to improve their skills-set, and generally adopt an enthusiastic approach to their work. However, Jerry, one of Travis's team members, has a fairly old-fashioned attitude to the relationship between boss and worker. Jerry holds the view that it is the manager's responsibility to create the right atmosphere for the team to flourish in; it is the manager's responsibility to build the team; it is the manager's responsibility to make improvements in the working arrangements, and so on. After all, in Jerry's mind that is what the boss gets paid to do. Further, Jerry sees his role as getting on and completing the tasks on his job description; anything else is doing extra work that is not necessary. As a result of these conflicting expectations, Jerry views these non-job roles as peripheral and a waste of time and energy. These incompatible unwritten expectations between Travis and Jerry result is some real frustration, despite the fact that both are, in their own ways, trying to accomplish what they understand to be their duty.

The mismatching psychological contracts in the above case can work in reverse too. For example, Mary is an employee with a belief that, as a member of the team, she will be consulted and involved in decision-making from time-to-time about work-related matters.

She wants to play her role in the team, to make a genuine contribution to the success of the organization, and grow and develop in the process. Mary believes Jenny, her manager, ought to share these roles with her team. But in this case, Jenny has a different understanding of the psychological contract. Jenny thinks that the lines of responsibility between herself and her team are very clear-cut. In Jenny's mind, her managerial role is broadly to make decisions and the subordinate's job is to complete the duties listed in their job description. But Mary finds it exasperating that Jenny is unwilling to engage the team in discussions about ways and means of being more efficient and effective as a team. Furthermore, Mary is keen to offer suggestions and discuss her ideas with Jenny. But Jenny is not at all receptive to any of her ideas and suggestions, let alone her approaches. Jenny doesn't believe in collaborative leadership. She views the managerial role as one of being clear, decisive, and forthright.

Besides, Jenny thinks her role is to make sure that workers are doing their job according to the specifications laid out in their job description. This is Jenny's idea of being professional and accountable. Mary on the other hand labels this approach as command and control. Here again, the reliance on a task-specific job description is really only going to exacerbate this misalignment in expectations. Similar to the earlier scenario, two well-intentioned people find themselves mutually locked out of a more productive working relationship because of conflicted psychological contracts, reinforced by the job description.

To navigate through the confusion caused from conflicting psychological contracts, I've developed two models that define and contrast the old and new psychological contracts. These two models are polar opposites; most organization cultures fall somewhere between the old and new. Anyway, by illustrating the diametrically opposite versions of the contract, we get a better sense of how dramatically the psychological contract is transforming in the world of work. Also, the models give some useful guideposts for evaluating the contracts in play in a workplace.

Traditional psychological contract

What exactly are the links between the traditional psychological contract and the job description? From the traditional psychological model, we can better understand the powerful part the job description plays in preserving this outdated model of the employment relationship. On the other hand, as you'll see, the old psychological contract reinforces the relevance of the job description. The job description and the old contract have a symbiotic relationship; they support each other inexorably.

Table 3.1 summarizes the attitudes of the employee and employer in the traditional employment relationship, based on eight shared values.

The left-hand column illustrates eight shared values based on research.[4] These values are the lynchpin of the traditional psychological contract. In the middle column, the eight brief descriptors summarize the expectations managers have of employees for the corresponding value. If an

TABLE 3.1   Traditional employment relationship model

Shared Value	Employee Mindset	Employer Mindset
Specialized Employment	*Work* in a clearly defined and specialized employment area.	*Offer* clearly defined and specialized employment opportunities.
Internal-Focus	*Follow* organizational policies and practices.	*Reinforce* the need to follow organizational policies and practices.
Job-Focus	*Fulfill* job requirements.	*Link* rewards and benefits to fulfilling job requirements.
Functional-Based Work	*Focus* on job functions.	*Structuring* work around functions.
Human Dispirit and Work	*Value* a stable and secure job.	*Offer* stable and secure jobs.
Loyalty	*Display* loyalty to the employer.	*Reward* employees who are loyal to the organization.
Training	*Commitment* to gain technical qualifications.	*Provide* opportunities for employees to develop technical skills.
Closed Information	*Comply* with managerial instructions.	*Provide* sufficient information for employees to do their job.

employee breaches any of these expectations, a traditional-minded manager will consider the contract dishonored. On the contrary, if employees' behavior is consistent with these mindsets, the value is strengthened. The right-hand column in Table 3.1 illustrates the typical outlook an employee has of managers. From the employee's perspective, if any of these expectations are broken, they will consider this a contract breach. On the other hand, if management's behavior is consistent with these mindsets, the values of the employment relationship are fortified. When these collective employee and management mindsets are put into effect, the traditional psychological contract is enacted. Should any behaviors by either partner be different to these expectations, the traditional psychological contract is broken temporarily or permanently.

Along with the performance review, the job description is one of the antiquated tools used to bolster the time-honored psychological contract I have illustrated in Table 3.1. I now want to explain more fully how the job description supports the eight shared values in the model.

Value of specialized employment

I will progress from the top of Table 3.1 to the bottom. The first value of *specialized employment* means working in a clearly defined and specialized employment area. The job description is designed to quarantine a job of work around a distinct set of tasks. In other words, the job description is intended to segment work around several functional areas. This is still how work is primarily structured in organizations. The job description helps to define the boundaries around the work people do in organizations. Through this mechanism of the specialization, it makes it easier to control, manage, and monitor the incumbent's job performance.

Value of internal-focus

The value of internal-focus is based on the concept of quality assurance, or QA as it is commonly referred to. The idea of QA extends back in history well before the Industrial Revolution to the Middle Ages. But the extensive division of labor and mechanization resulting from the Industrial Revolution, made it possible for workers to control the quality of their own products. The Industrial Revolution led to a system in which large groups of people performing a specialized type of work were grouped together under the supervision of a foreman who was appointed to control the quality of work manufactured.

The task-based job description became a vehicle for promoting QA. The document refers to, explains, and reinforces standardized organizational policies and practices. The thrust of the job description is largely to provide direction for employees to follow internal processes and procedures. QA's ultimate aim is to prevent mistakes or defects in manufactured products and avoid problems when delivering solutions or services to customers. And the job description is a way of standardizing the work employees do.

Value of job-focus

The value of *job-focus* is essentially about satisfying the requirements of the job. The rationale for this value – at least from a managerial perspective – is that increasing organizational performance resides at the job level. When it comes to job-focus as a value, employees expect managers to reward them for exceeding their KPIs. By collectively elevating job performance, with rewards and benefits, the popular argument is that this leads to increasing the total output of the organization. The idea of "systems thinking" has basically discredited this argument. But the job description, focusing on the job, pays little attention to the interdependencies of systems and processes, the area where real productivity gains can be made.

Value of functional-based work

The value of *functional-based work* is about structuring and focusing the work that needs doing around a set of clearly defined functions, often referred to as divisions, departments, and sections. Each function has a distinct identity and specific skills-set. With a functional structure, the work identity of an employee resides with these functions. For instance, when asked where they work, an employee may respond with, "I work in the marketing department." The job description supports a functional-based structure; it describes the interrelationship between a particular job and the department it serves.

Value of human dispirit and work

The value of *human dispirit and work* is to do with offering and valuing stable and secure jobs that aren't necessarily exciting or autonomous. For many workers still, a clearly defined, reasonably predictable, and easy to follow job is more appealing than an ambiguous, unpredictable, and ever-changing job. A well-established method to generate stability and certainty in what is required in a workplace is a job analysis, the precursor to a job description. The job description endeavors to standardize work into small, easy to understand component parts that are highly predict-able and somewhat repetitive.

Value of loyalty

In the context of the employment relationship, the value of *loyalty* is based on the employee displaying allegiance to their current employer in exchange for a stable job and good working conditions. From the employer's perspective, the value of loyalty assumes that by rewarding an employee with the provision of a secure job and reasonable working conditions, this entitles them to loyalty from the employee. Loyalty to an employer is rewarded in other ways too. For instance, I have witnessed several instances of employees receiving pay bonuses or recognition from business owners, such as a large plasma color television for 20-odd years of service in the same company. Employment stability is neatly packaged as a concept called a *job*. The job description gives a certain amount of legitimacy by carving out a need in a workplace based upon a job construct. For this chunk of work, sculptured into a formatted job description, the employee is supposed to feel obliged to reciprocate by staying employed in that organization for some time.

Value of training

The value of *training* is based on building employees' technical capabilities to discharge the task obligations laid out in the job description. Training as a value is about the employee committing to gaining technical qualifications and the employer providing opportunities for employees to develop technical skills. Technical or production-centered training (see Chapter 2) and its importance are amplified by the task-related job specification and its accompanying job description.

Value of closed information

Closed information as a value is the provision of sufficient – but no more – information for employees to carry out their job duties. The manager provides enough information for the employee to do their job, and in return the employee is expected to comply with managerial instructions. The familiar catch cry, "you'll be told on a need to know basis" is part of this contractual arrangement. An important vehicle for information about the work that needs doing is of course contained in the job description. This document is supposed to contain sufficient information for the employee to communicate what is expected of them in their job. The manager then holds the employee to account for meeting the KPIs in the job description.

As you can no doubt gather from these brief descriptors of the eight values of the old employment contract, the job description has a key part to play in not only sustaining, but strengthening the outdated employment relationship. In sum, the job description is the vehicle for defining the boundaries of employee responsibility around a set of tasks (specialized employment). The job description supports a focus on internal systems and processes (internal-focus). It assists in structuring the organization around a set of functions (functional-based work). The job description conveys a feeling of stability and certainty, if not excitement (human dispirit and work). The packaging of work as a job – presented in a visual format of a document – is appealing, and offers an employee something tangible. It induces the employee to display loyalty to the employer (loyalty). The job description highlights the need to be technically competent (training). And it contains just enough information to hold the employee accountable for achieving certain results (closed information). The job description – apart from being the backbone of most HRM practices – is one of the main inhibitors of transforming to a more dynamic psychological contract between employee and employer.

In the next chapter we will continue this discussion, looking at the new employment relationship and considering how inadequate the job description is in its current form to accommodate a new psychological contract necessary for the changing workplace.

The **Top 10** Key Points …

1. Working in unison, this obsolete psychological contract has reinforced the relevance of the job description well beyond its usefulness. The job description and the traditional psychological contract have a symbiotic relationship.

2. The job description is designed to quarantine a job of work around a clearly defined set of tasks.

3. The task-based job description became a vehicle for promoting QA and the value of internal-focus.

4. The job description is central to a focus on the job.

5. The job description supports this emphasis on structuring organizations around functions.

6. The job description endeavors to standardize work into small, easy to understand component parts.

7 The job description gives a certain amount of legitimacy to the idea of a valued job. For this chunk of work, sculptured into an attractive job description, the employee may feel obliged to reciprocate by staying employed in that organization for several years.

8 Technical- or production-centered training and its importance is amplified by the task-related job specification and its accompanying job description.

9 The job description is supposed to contain sufficient information for the employee to do their job. The manager then holds the employee accountable for meeting the terms in this document.

10 The job description – apart from being the backbone of most HRM practices – is one of the main inhibitors of transcending to a more dynamic psychological contract between employee and employer.

The Job Description and the New Contract

A culture supported by the new employment relationship model is a culture based on and sustained by a wider and deeper range of competencies than those belonging to the task-related job description.

Josh has been thinking long and hard. As part of the latest workplace agreement, the company is about to embark on a program of job redesign for all non-salaried employees. Multi-skilling will be the major emphasis of this job redesign. The goal is to enhance flexibility, efficiency, and job satisfaction.

In keeping with employees' wishes and with the national trend towards industrial democracy, this job redesign will be undertaken "participatively." Managers will be responsible for leading the job redesign in their own departments in consultation with their team members. They are to ensure that all employees have a fair input into the process, that equal employment opportunity, health, safety, and welfare issues take top priority, and that a net 3 per cent gain in output results from the job restructuring program. Measures of each department's success will include attendance rates, number of grievances registered, output, production costs, and other benchmark measures of efficiency and quality.

As Josh rolls this around in his mind, he can see some obvious benefits for employees. They will have greater variety of tasks to accomplish and therefore learn more skills and hopefully derive more job satisfaction; they will have a greater say in how their department operates (he tries to give that to them anyway); they will have better career opportunities; and expectantly, they will have better jobs. Depending on how the redesign takes shape, they will probably even have the opportunity to undertake complete projects and have more responsibility and decision-making in their work.

And Josh can see plenty of benefits to the company, apart from those stated in the workplace agreement. Multi-skilled staff, improved occupational health and safety, better and easier recruitment and retention due to increased levels of job satisfaction, more effective use of technology, improved staff morale ... it sounds too good to be true! Josh wonders: What is the downside of all this?[1]

If you weren"t familiar with the term before, I trust you now know what the *psychological contract* means and what the eight shared values are between employee and manager of the old contract. Travelling to the opposite end of the psychological contract continuum, I want to take a look at the new psychological contract in this chapter. By familiarizing yourself with the other end of the spectrum, you can juxtapose the two polar models of the psychological contract. This comparative analysis adds further weight to my argument of the futility and counter-productiveness of persevering with the job description.

Just as I introduced you to the traditional employment relationship model in Chapter 2, I want to do the same thing in this chapter and share with you the new employment relationship model.

New psychological contract

I have defined one end of the psychological contract continuum in Table 3.1 (*see* page 56). Now we go to the other end of the gamut to consider a diametrically opposite model of the contract. The research-based new employment relationship model takes into account the changing dynamics in the world of work and the new challenges for organizations and employees to now survive and thrive in a VUCA marketplace. A workplace revolution began in the 1980s;[2] it profoundly altered the expectations employees and employers have of each other. The new model serves as a reference point to capture the essence of these changing beliefs. A culture characterized by the shared values of the new employment relationship model is a culture that embraces a range of non-job roles and competencies to supplement existing job competencies.

Table 4.1 illustrates the eight shared values and the corresponding expectations employees and managers have of each other in the new contract.

Although the new and the traditional employment relationship models provide the polar benchmarks of the spectrum of the psychological contract, there are similarities in the structure of the two models. Both frameworks

TABLE 4.1　New employment relationship model

Shared Value	Employee Mindset	Employer Mindset
Flexible Deployment	*Willingness* to work in a variety of organizational roles and settings.	*Encourage* employees to work in other organizational roles.
Customer-Focus	*Serve* the customer before your manager.	*Provide* information, skills, and incentives to focus externally.
Performance-Focus	*Focus* on what you do, not where you work.	*Link* rewards and benefits with performance rather than organizational dependency.
Project-Based Work	*Accept* yourself as a project-based worker rather than a function-based employee.	*Structuring* work around projects rather than organizational functions.
Human Spirit and Work	*Valuing* work that is meaningful.	*Provide* work (wherever possible) that is meaningful.
Commitment	*Commit* to assisting the organization in achieving its outcomes.	*Commit* to assisting employees in achieving their personal objectives.
Learning and Development	*Commit* to lifelong learning.	*Enter* into a partnership for employee development.
Open Information	*Willing* to show enterprise and initiative.	*Providing* employees with access to a wide range of information.

are based on eight shared values. The models describe a set of collective expectations employees and employers have of each other in their working relationship. Behaviors that are consistent or inconsistent with these typical beliefs about their partner in the employment relationship will either reinforce or challenge the shared value in the left-hand column.

It would be helpful to briefly explain the contrasting values in the two models. The job description – as I pointed out earlier – is an instrument underpinning and strengthening the old contract. Simply put, the job description is the backbone of the old psychological contract. Allow me to illustrate how inadequately equipped the job description is to accommodate this new psychological contract. I will draw attention to each of the eight changing values in both models.

Specialized employment to Flexible deployment

In the old contract, the employee expected their manager to provide a specialized job and clearly-defined description of that job. In exchange for this, the manager expected the employee to complete that job according to the job description. The job description is perfectly suited for the value of specialized employment. But the new value of *flexible deployment* holds an entirely different set of beliefs.

In terms of flexible deployment, the expectation of the manager is that the employee is prepared to work in a variety of organizational positions and deploy their skills-set in a host of work situations. Employees too expect their manager to provide them with employment opportunities that are varied and flexible. The employee wants to flexibly deploy their competencies in a variety of organizational settings and conditions; they are prepared and willing to learn how to adapt or deploy their current skills-set.

A job description, as we know, is supposed to be tailored for a specific job. So, deploying the job-specific competencies to other work contexts is counter to the idea of the job description. In other words, flexibly deploying a particular skills-set is using these job skills in circumstances outside the specifications of the job. For example, an engineer specializing in civil construction invited to work as part of a large-scale, multi-disciplinary project team, needs to be open to learning a new set of competencies. The engineer must learn to apply their specialized skills in a different way. The job description, with its obvious specialization orientation, is incongruous for the value of flexible deployment.

To be able to apply a set of skills in diverse ways is a competency in itself. A flexibly deployed employee needs to acquire certain non-job competencies to enable them to adapt to new situations. For instance, the employee must be open to the idea of developing themselves to be fully capable of deploying their skills-set. Being in a state of continuously growing and developing one's skill-set is part of the non-job roles framework. But the job description – with its onus of specialization – doesn't encourage development through deployment.

Internal-focus to Customer-focus

Under the old contract, the employee wants their manager to provide them with clear policies and processes to follow. In return for this, the manager wants the employee to faithfully follow these policies and procedures. So the value of internal-focus from the manager's perspective is essentially about reinforcing the organization's set policies and procedures. The manager then expects the employee to enthusiastically follow these practices. The value of internal-focus is really about QA, as we discussed in the previous chapter.

In complete contrast, the employee's expectation in relation to the value of *customer-focus* is for their manager to provide them with information, skills, and processes to focus externally, not internally, on the needs of the customer. In exchange, the manager wants the employee to focus their attention on the needs of the customer. The new value of *customer-focus* is more outcome-driven than process-driven.

But as we know, the job description calls attention to the adherence of internal processes and practices. Employee success under the old contract is often the result of observing and respecting organizational systems and practices. Yet, to be good with customers, the employee needs more than a willingness and capacity to follow internal processes and procedures. For example, the ability to problem-solve and think "outside the box" are useful competencies to have when dealing with unexpected customer requests. Problem-solving and critical thinking are elements of the non-job role of innovation and continuous improvement. The ability to problem-solve and be agile is increasingly more relevant with customer dealings. The hyper-competitive global economy and the ever-expanding array of customer requests and preferences means that "dotting i's and crossing t's" internally is "not going to cut it" any more with the fickle and picky customer.

As I pointed out in the last chapter, the job description is more suited to supporting the value of internal-focus than the value of customer-focus. Briefly, the need to be more flexible and responsive to the whims of the modern-day customer involves competencies beyond dutifully following internal procedures and processes. A role description on the other hand, encourages a wider range of competencies better suited to responding to a more complex marketplace.

A T   T H E   C O A L   F A C E   ...

The changing customer is like the changing employee

Rosabeth Kanter made this observation about customers in her well-documented article, *Mastering Change*: "Study after study around the world shows that employees today are less loyal, less committed and more mobile than ever before. In industry after industry power is systematically shifting away from those who produce goods and services. The customer, like the employee, is less loyal, more fickle and therefore demands a different kind of response from organizations: more flexibility, greater innovation, more attention to where the customer's needs are heading in the future, rather than expecting them to take today's goods and services."[3]

Job-focus to Performance-focus

In the past, managers had a belief that everything done by the employee, other than the literal tasks in the job description, was considered a waste of time and diversion of labor. And so the responsibility of the manager was to provide rewards and benefits with the achievement of job-based KPIs. Under the old contract, the employee wants clarity and direction on their job obligations from their manager; they view non-job roles as a distraction from getting the task done.

Under the new contract, the value is *performance-focus*, taking on a broader interpretation of work which is more than job performance. The manager expects the employee to support the organization in reaching its strategic direction; this requires a combination of job and non-job contributions. From the employee's perspective, the manager's role is to provide rewards and incentives to performing the job and non-job dimensions of work. As we discussed in Chapter 2, doing a job and performing at work are not necessarily the same thing.

Performing at work in the 21st century is multi-dimensional; it covers the job role and a range of non-job roles. These non-job roles are not covered, or at least, not covered in the same level of detail as the job role in the job description. With a heavy weighting on technical competencies, the second generation job description doesn't ordinarily promote the non-job dimension of work. Performance in the old contract is defined narrowly around a cluster of task-specific KPIs. The focus is on the job and not performance.

Functional-based work to Project-based work

Employees under the old contract see it as the manager's responsibility to structure work around organizational functions. This hierarchical structure organizes employees with similar skills-set to work together; it gives them a functional identity in the business. The manager believes the employees' energies are best utilized by wholly concentrating them within these homogeneous work pods. But the silo work structure is too inflexible to respond straightaway to the demands of the warp speed marketplace. So it is unsurprising that *project-based work* is fast becoming the dominant organizing structure. While functions are relatively permanent organizing structures, project teams come and go, depending on the just-in-time needs of the market.

The employee with a new employment relationship mindset wants their manager to value and utilize their skills-set. They are open to the possibilities of participating in a variety of short- and long-term projects and contractual assignments. The attraction for the employee is working with a variety of stakeholders in multi-disciplinary teams, where they can deploy and develop their skills and boost their employability.

The progressive manager, with a similar mindset, encourages the employee to take these options when they are offered and view their work identity as portable and not tied to a functional silo. The organization of work is far more flexible and less rigidly structured when focused on projects rather than functions. Project-based work is more responsive to a turbulent global marketplace.

But the problem is this: Job descriptions are the blueprint for a functional-based job. The job description assumes a hierarchical organizing structure. Further, it captures the reporting regime within the section, department, or division. This work document is unsuitable for work structured around cross-functional projects that involve a wider range of competencies than the functional specifications of a job.

For instance, to work effectively in a project team, the employee has to be a team player. Being a team player in this context means placing the overall needs of the project ahead of their own personal needs. In a functional position, the employee can afford – and even, legitimize – being self-absorbed from time-to-time. The job-holder can be selfish and justify this on the basis of attending to their "priorities" embedded in the job description. The functional focus of the job description discourages the cultivation of cross-functional communication and teamwork.

Human dispirit and work to Human spirit and work

In the old contract, the employee favors stable and
secure employment over exciting jobs with no job
security. So the employee expects the organization to offer them a secure job. The traditional manager also believes that a steady
and protected job is what an employee
values above all else. Now, the
employee – particularly the
younger worker – wants and
expects the organization to
offer them meaningful work
assignments and opportunities;
they are seeking work that engages
their "heart and mind."

Now, the employee – particularly the younger worker – wants and expects the organization to offer them meaningful work assignments and opportunities; they are seeking work that engages their "heart and mind."

The manager's thinking is transforming too. They are more likely now to
appreciate that employees value work that has meaning; that workers
have little interest in a stable, boring job for life. This shifting employee
and employer belief about the role work plays in people's lives means the
pendulum is swinging from a shared value of human dispirit and work to
human spirit and work.

Finding real meaning from work is probably more than doing a bundle of
prescribed tasks, over-and-over again. Meaning from work can be derived
from many different sources. For instance, personal and professional
development can hold meaning for lots of employees. For others, inves-
tigating and implementing new ways of doing work-related tasks easier,
better, faster, more accurately, and so on, can be rewarding. Developing
friendships and building strong working relationships can inject a sense
of meaning into an otherwise mundane work environment. From my
experience, there are limitless ways people find meaning from the work
they do. But it's fair to say that a lot of meaningful work experiences are
not necessarily directly tied to the KRAs in the job description.

It is worth remembering that the job description was not created to help the job-holder find meaning in their work. The job description was put in place to direct, control, monitor, and evaluate the work of the employee. It also furnishes the conventional need of the employee for stability and security. The role description alternatively heralds more scope for the employee to contribute openly to experiences that can inject a sense of engagement and meaning in their work.

Loyalty to Commitment

The original expectation of the employee was to be remunerated for abiding by the organization's systems and processes. In exchange for the rewards of employment, the employee demonstrates their loyalty by not seeking employment elsewhere, particularly with the company's competitors. In the old contract, the manager wants the employee to respect the way things are done in the business, without question, and not look for work elsewhere. In short, the manager expects the employee to be loyal to their employer in exchange for giving them a job for life.

In the new psychological contract, the value of *commitment* is based in part on the employee wanting the employer to support them in achieving their personal goals. In exchange, the employee offers themselves and their skills-set to assist in the achievement of the strategic direction of the business. The manager's response can be summed up as; *I am providing you with career development opportunities because you are helping me to achieve our strategic direction*.

The role description offers more scope than the job description to demonstrate commitment. For instance, from the employer's perspective, the non-job roles framework offers additional ways the organization can explicitly commit to furthering an employee's career goals. More specifically, the organization can obligate to support employees in career development programs, whether it is learning and development opportunities, assessment centers, or other offerings. This is one of many possibilities for the employer to show commitment to the employee.

Alternatively, commitment can be demonstrated by the employee through positive non-job behaviors. For example, an employee can help a business to streamline their IT systems and practices. The business decides to reciprocate by sponsoring that employee to attend a training program to further their vocational aspirations. Commitment to improving the business is followed by the business committing to "improving" the employee! That's how the value of commitment should work in the new psychological contract.

In addition, two-way commitment is a more pragmatic and constructive working arrangement than one based on the fuzzy notion of loyalty. Demonstrating commitment in a relationship is firstly knowing what the other party needs; and secondly, satisfying that need. The role description expands the possibilities open for reciprocal commitment to embrace the job and non-job dimensions. So commitment from the employee and organization can be displayed across several non-job areas of performance.

As we'll discuss in Part II, KPIs for non-job roles are documented, so it becomes clearer what the employee can do (and not do) to meet the changing expectations of the manager. And the organization can commit to supporting the employee to perform their non-job roles. So, briefly, the non-job dimension potentially strengthens the value of commitment between individual and organization.

Training to Learning and development

In a "them and us" working relationship, the employee expects the manager to provide them with adequate technical training so that they can complete the tasks in their job description competently. Equally, the manager, with the benefit derived from good production-centered training, expects the employee to attain the job-related KPIs. These are the beliefs that support the shared value of training.

The value of training is a vehicle for improving the job-holders' capacity to complete their job specification. But the difference with a shared value of *learning and development* sustaining the new contract is that this value includes non-technical learning opportunities as well as technical training. So learning and development encompasses a wider range of experiences and opportunities.

Non-technical learning includes the person-centered and problem-centered approaches we covered in Chapter 2. This progression from training to learning and development is largely attributable to the manager embracing the cliché that *the most important resources in an organization are its people*. Although a cliché, it is nonetheless true. This belief has eventually become well-established in the workplace.

This realization brings with it the notion that organizations have an obligation to develop the whole person, and not just the job-holder. By developing the person beyond their task responsibilities, there is an expectation that the employee will contribute to organizational performance with positive non-job behavior. To match this changing managerial belief, the organization needs to take a whole-of-person approach to learning and development.

As we discussed in Chapter 2, production-centered or technical training is the mainstay of the job-centric workplace. Unlike the job description, the role description promotes the idea of non-technical HRD, or person-centered and problem-centered learning. For example, consider the development of new ideas in an enterprise. What can be done to encourage the contribution and expansion of practical ideas and suggestions? In a *hackathon*[4] – the latest trend in innovation and continuous improvement – participants, who are generally groups of employees, may be exposed to a creative thinking workshop beforehand. The production-centered, person-centered, and problem-centered approaches to learning and development are all relevant in the role-centric organization.

The value of learning and development brings into play a more holistic view of HRD. But the job description, with its concentration on job-specific activity, perpetuates the idea that technical training is the "be all and end all." This job-focus can asphyxiate the non-technical dimension of learning and development.

Closed information to Open information

Under the old contract, the manager believes that – given sufficient information – the employee ought to be able to carry out their duties. The employee too is prepared to follow instructions with the right amount of information; they don't expect – nor want – any more information than is necessary to do their job. Closed information is essentially providing sufficient information for the employee to do their jobs and, in exchange, the employee complies with managerial instructions. This sums up the old value of closed information.

But under the new contract, the manager and employee have a completely different set of beliefs. The manager wants the employee to display their initiative when dealing with an "out-of-the-box" workplace dilemma. However, to be enterprising in these unusual circumstances, employees need more information than they usually get under the old contract. Put simply, the employee needs the same perspective as their boss to be enterprising; to have the same perspective, they need the same information. Generally speaking, the employee now looks forward to being informed about a wider range of work-related matters than in the past. To confidently display initiative at the right time, in the right place, and in the right way, the employee needs to know a lot more than just how to do their job. Displaying enterprising behavior at the "coal face" requires an open and trusting channel of communication between management and workforce. This is the basis of the value of *open information*.

Occasionally, the term, "displaying initiative" is mentioned in the job description. But paradoxically, displaying initiative usually means going outside the bounds of the standard job specification. In workplaces where a "them and us" culture prevails, very little or no initiative takes place. On the rare occasion that an employee musters the courage to display their initiative, it is not always appreciated, especially when the results are less than satisfactory! Being enterprising under the old contract can actually be career limiting! The job description is designed ultimately to promote compliance and standardization, not encourage initiative and inventiveness. The role description is more apt at supporting the value of open information.

It should be apparent to you by now the profound difference between the old and new psychological contracts, particularly the beliefs the employee and manager have of each other. What's more, these radically different constructs form two diametrically opposite sets of shared values; these values represent the book-ends of the psychological contract spectrum. The job description underpins each of the eight values of the traditional employment relationship. While the job description is suitable for supporting the old contract, it is manifestly unsuitable for supporting the values of the new contract.

How closely your organization is aligned to either the new or old model indicates the level of attachment or detachment organizational members have to the job description. The closer the employment relationship mirrors the eight shared values of the new employment relationship model, the less attachment and relevance the job description has in the enterprise. In reverse, the more bonded you are to the job description and challenging it is to let go of it, the more difficult it is likely to be to transform from an old to new psychological contract.

With the task-focus of the job description, the manager understandably evaluates the employee's contribution against the job task KPIs. The employee evaluates their own performance this way too. It is therefore often the case that the employee, with justification, thinks and sometimes says: "If it's not on my job description, I'm not required to do it." But, as we have discussed: Performing at work is more than what is expressed in the job description. For an employee to perform in today's warp speed global economy they must go further than meeting or exceeding their task-based KPIs. If you're still not convinced, then consider why it is – as I mentioned in very beginning of Chapter 1 – that most job descriptions have a "statement of other duties" disclaimer at the end of the document. What is the compulsion then, to include this disclaimer that says something along the lines of: "... and any other duties deemed necessary by your supervisor"? Clearly, it means there are other performance factors not included in the job description.

Since the height of the scientific management movement's influence over 100 years ago, managers have used a variety of formats to carve out the task duties of employees. For the most part, controlling work by clarifying the job and task competencies of the employee has been highly effective. But we are now using an old tool for work that's unrecognizable from the Ford assembly line. Identifying and expressing the contribution an employee is supposed to make in an organizational-setting is still relevant today, but we need a new tool.

Together with the archaic performance review, the job description is an artifact of the 20th-century command and control management mindset. These management tools are holding us back; we need to let go of them and come up with a new set of tools for our HR toolkit.

This brings us to the end of Part I. In Part II, we look more closely at the "other" dimension of work I refer to as non-job roles. In particular, we examine four non-job roles employees are increasingly expected to perform as part of their work, and consider why they are more important than ever in the performance-focused organization.

The **Top 10** Key Points ...

1. The research-based new employment relationship model takes into account the changing dynamics in the world of work and the new requirements for organizations and employees to survive and thrive from an HRM perspective.

2. The job description, with its orientation towards specialized employment, is incongruous for developing a value of flexible deployment in an organizational setting.

3. The job description is more readily suited to supporting the value of internal-focus than the value of customer-focus.

4. The way the job description is written, with its emphasis on job tasks, doesn't promote the expansion and development of important performance-related, non-job roles.

5. The job description is unsuitable for describing the work that needs doing in a project-based environment.

6. The job description was not designed to create meaningful work; it was put in place to direct, control, monitor, and evaluate the work of the employee.

7. As a tool of exchange between employer and employee, the role description has more scope than the job description and therefore greater opportunities for exercising shared commitment.

8. Dissimilar to the job description, the role description promotes the idea of non-technical HRD.

9. The job description is designed ultimately to encourage compliance and standardization, not initiative and inventiveness.

10. A new psychological contract between employer and employee is taking shape. We need a new set of tools in our HR toolkit.

part II

Non-Job Roles

5

The Non-Job Roles Framework

Despite the endless supply of articles, the mountain of books, omnipresent blogs, and annual conferences on workplace performance, most performance management systems are still disappointing and substandard.

Greg Kean is considered to be one of the brightest recruits in a large and reputable engineering consultancy firm. He graduated from university six years ago with excellent grades and has always been a keen and willing employee, eager to get ahead.

Because of his ability, work ethic, clear thinking, and organizing capability, the firm promoted him to the position of manager. He has a team of five. When Greg was promoted, he became more determined than ever to show the business unit manager his leadership capabilities. His level of motivation was very high and he decided to make a clean sweep of his area of responsibility and really "smarten up the act" of his team.

Prior to Greg's promotion, his team had a reputation as an "easy does-it" team. The work was done and – by-and-large – done well, meeting client and project deadlines mostly. However, as far as Greg could see, the previous manager really didn't "manage" at all.

So in Greg Kean went, tightening up on systems and procedures, making sure they were followed, ensuring lunch breaks weren't extended, continually monitoring everyone's work, handing out jobs and assignments each morning, and generally ruling with the proverbial "iron fist." Plenty of time to get to know the team later, thought Greg, once I have established the new order of things around here!

Now, four months later, the most experienced engineer has left to join a competing firm, another is openly looking for a new job, and the team is no longer functioning as a unit. The four who are left seem to have withdrawn their cooperation, display no initiative, and do only what Greg tells them to do.

Greg's unit manager has decided it is time to have a chat with Greg about his poor leadership performance. He looked over Greg's job description and noticed that it doesn't mention anything about leadership; it was very specific, however, about the technical requirements of the position. Greg's boss was faced with a dilemma: How could he constructively criticize Greg's leadership of his team when nothing is mentioned in the job description and Greg has never had any formal leadership training?[1]

Organizational work that employees engage in is two-dimensional. The job description documents one of these two dimensions: The technical or task-related dimension. As I discussed in Part I, the non-job dimension – the other dimension – is not covered in any substantial way, if at all, in the job description. This is why the job description should be replaced; it doesn't record *all* the work employees are suppose to perform. In other words, the task-specific job description doesn't comprehensively cover all employee responsibilities.

The transformative changes in the workplace since the mid-1980s have bought into question work performance and what it does and doesn't involve. Was job performance in the 1950s the same as it is today? Undoubtedly not. But the job description format has stayed reasonably constant since the 1950s; it is still almost exclusively focused on job-task activity.

Although some evolution has taken place, the job description is still based on the technical or job dimension of performance. As we discussed in Chapter 1, the first generation job description is basically a breakdown of the tasks the incumbent is expected to do. The second generation one considers the competencies required to do these tasks effectively. A role description adds another dimension; it includes the non-job dimension to the job dimension of work.

On the assumption that the job description is comprehensively and clearly drafted, it already captures one dimension; the job dimension. My view is that a performance-focus, as distinct from a job-focus, incorporates at least four non-job roles; these non-job roles are covered in detail later in Part II. By elevating the status of what I refer to as the non-job roles framework in the work documentation, it is the first important step in changing from a job-focus to a performance-focus. With the role description I advocate, the employee has five roles to perform: one job role and four non-job roles.

Job description, role description, and various definitions

There's a plethora of terms and processes used around the world to capture the essence of what someone does at work. But overall, the document itself is commonly referred to as a job or position description. It would be impossible (and pointless) to cover all these labels and meanings. But I'll touch on a few here. In the United Kingdom, there is the job description, role profile, and person specification linked to a competency framework. In the United States, most organizations have a competency framework which integrates the knowledge, skills, judgment, and attributes people need for the various roles they have in the organization. Australia has a competency-based approach also, particularly in the public sector. In many cases, however, the document that reflects what a person should do and contribute as a job-holder is poorly written and inconclusive, irrespective of the terms or frameworks used.

Generally speaking, irrespective of the country, or industry, the job description defines a set of specific tasks and responsibilities that are performed by the incumbent. Particular tasks are typically expressed in terms of outputs; for example, *to maintain filing and record systems*. The second generation job description spells out a set of behaviors or competencies needed by the job-holder; it characteristically includes employee traits required for competent performance of a particular job. Although a job description describes and focuses on the job itself, it rarely includes the four non-job roles I intend to cover in subsequent chapters.

In my definition of the role description, an additional layer of accountability is covered. Apart from the tasks and responsibilities – the technical requirements of a job – the role description contains key non-job roles too. These non-job roles are covered in as much detail as the job role, with competencies, associated elements, and KPIs. The role description redefines the duties and responsibilities of the employee into a series of roles, including the job role.

Non-job performance

The employee's performance is based on fulfilling their organizational role as well as their job tasks and competencies. I referred to this modification as the third generation (see Figure 1.1 on p. 24). From an organization development perspective, the non-job roles the employee performs well, not too well, or poorly can be as impactful to the performance of an enterprise as the execution of job-tasks. It is now widely recognized that roles such as maintaining a positive and enthusiastic attitude, displaying teamwork, developing one's work skills, and contributing to improving the way the workplace functions are vitally important to organizational performance. Yet these four competencies are non-job specific and as such, rarely, if ever, get covered in detail in an employee's job description.

Nevertheless, there is a growing belief that all employees have a responsibility to be enterprising and enthusiastic, work in teams, grow and develop their capabilities, and look for better ways to improve organizational efficiencies. But this commonly held view has been an implicit expectation, rather than an explicitly documented declaration.

Despite this inherent and widely held understanding, managers pay more attention to task-related behaviors and less attention to non-job behaviors. By giving more attention to impactful non-job behaviors, leaders are encouraging non-job competencies that facilitate organizational performance beyond task-specific achievements.

In particular, organizational performance can be improved by the morale-lifting behavior of being positive and enthusiastic in adversity, sacrificing self-interest for the sake of the team, learning and applying a new skill on the job, and coming up with a new and better way of doing something that benefits the business. Recognition from the manager, and awareness from the employee of these organizational roles, will begin the process of changing the prevailing psychological contract from a job-focus to a performance-focus. Everyone benefits from a performance-based organizational culture. Organizational leaders have a perpetual interest in more fully engaging the hearts and minds of employees. Employees can value-add to their current job and improve their employability when exercising the full extent of their non-job roles. The customer or end-user benefits from better products and services. A more profitable company means that shareholders and owners are happier too.

Although the job description limits employee contributions to job-specific behaviors, managers ironically want to employ people who willingly and continually add value over and above their job role. Further, managers value non-job behaviors regardless of technical skill, hierarchical status, or length of tenure. For ambitious employees, this means that notable organizational contributions outside the scope of their job description, such as the non-job roles mentioned so far, are potentially career enhancing. On the assumption that an employee's job performance is at least up-to-scratch, positive non-job behavior adds another facet to their work performance. Positive non-job behavior contributes to the success of both the individual and organization.

In the past, employees who stuck stringently to the letter of their job description were held in high regard for exhibiting a reliable and conscientious approach to their job. The opposite is true now: Managers, embracing the values of the new psychological contract, want employees to be enterprising; this means displaying proactive, positive behavior over and above the scope of the job description.

Despite the endless supply of articles, the mountain of books, omnipresent blogs, and annual conferences on workplace performance, most performance management systems are still disappointing and substandard. These systems more often than not ignore – or only pay lip service to – aspects of work performance that are not specifically job-related. The best illustration of a poor system is what have been – and still are – the conventional building blocks of organizational performance: The job specification and job description.

Naturally, non-job related performance criteria needs the same rigor applied to it as job-specific tasks. I understand that some organizations have what they refer to as a *role description*, which generally amounts to a list of bullet points as an appendage to the main task-focused document. Take for instance the following unquestionably valuable non-job behaviors:

- Making practical suggestions for workplace improvements.
- Being a positive and enthusiastic organizational citizen.
- Displaying initiative to delight a customer with prudent but extraordinary customer service.

I have never yet seen these characteristics mentioned in detail, with specific and unambiguous KPIs, in a job description. And if they are mentioned, they are done so vaguely with statements such as: *We encourage employees to offer their suggestions at work* or perhaps more forthrightly: *You are expected to be a team player*. In any case, these sorts of statements – if they are included at all – are listed toward the end of the job document, with an absence of detail as to what these behaviors mean in practice, or how they will be assessed.

And so it is because of these concerns that I want to advocate a broader interpretation of performance that goes further than job-specific behaviors identified in first and generation job descriptions. This framework supports and reinforces desirable workplace accomplishment that is not necessarily job-related. What's more, I want to overhaul what I see as the key deficiency in the performance management system – the job description – and replace it with a role description.

Figure 5.1 illustrates this more expansive framework of work performance.

The second generation job description covers the *job role, tasks, competencies,* and *KPIs* illustrated on the left-hand side of Figure 5.1. In the role description, the job is conceptualized as the job role. The arrangement on the right-hand side, consisting of *non-job roles, elements,* competencies, and *KPIs,* is related to non-job behaviors. In effect, this means that the role description, as I have mentioned several times, consists of five roles – one job role and four non-job roles.

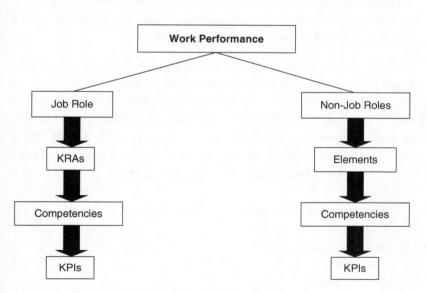

FIGURE 5.1 / **Model of work performance**

Contextual performance

Contextual performance covers multiple sub-dimensions of work, such as attitude and enthusiasm, teamwork, growth and development, and innovation and continuous improvement. Although multi-dimensional models of performance – including job and non-job dimensions – have been introduced in some companies, they lack a consistent and unifying framework across the general workforce. Without a common structure, there is little direction for managers to choose which dimensions of contextual performance to include (or exclude) from a performance review system. This lack of a clear framework leads to the default position covering unambiguous job-related criterion only.

But in truth, all organizational positions consist of core or central tasks and contextual behaviors. In the past, performance at work has neglected contextual indicators for a host of reasons, such as the absence of objective criteria. This is despite widespread acknowledgment that these intangible aspects of work are integral to overall performance. Therefore performance systems that only evaluate job competencies are incomplete and consequently deficient, particularly against the backdrop of the VUCA global marketplace.

To reinforce my point about the relevance of fully documenting contextual performance criteria, consider this question: *What are the competencies that employers value most in employees?* A list of the ten most valued job competencies has been compiled from over 40 studies of medium- and large-scale employers, primarily in the United States but also in other countries such as Australia, France, Singapore, and the United Kingdom. These top ten job competencies are:[2]

1. Enthusiasm/positive attitude.
2. Good communication skills.
3. Self-motivated/initiative.
4. Honest.
5. Must like people.
6. Persistent.

7. Able to work in a team.
8. Good organizational skills/work well under pressure.
9. Willing to learn.
10. Dependable/hardworking.

All ten of these competencies are valuable in any employment context; they are applicable in professional, semi-professional, and non-professional vocations; blue collar or white collar; indoor or outdoor; and traditional or non-traditional industries. When recruiting potential employees, these are competencies we look for, apart from technical qualifications and experience. But once a person is selected and commences employment, these non-job specific competencies aren't explicitly and consistently recognized and rewarded.

The number of potential roles employees can take on at work is limitless. Some are consciously performed and others unconsciously carried out. Some are relevant, some not. Some take a split second to execute, some are ongoing. Some are appreciated, some not. Some are rewarded, some not. An important question then is: *What are the relevant and universally acceptable roles employees can perform in organizations, apart from carrying out their job role?*

Four universally acceptable roles

As I've mentioned several times, there are four non-job roles that are becoming increasingly important in any workplace. Together these four roles constitute the non-job roles framework. These roles include:

- A positive mental attitude and enthusiasm role.
- A team role.
- A career development role.
- An innovator and continuous improvement role.

Reflecting on the above-mentioned list of ten job competencies for a moment, there are obviously many other roles – apart from the four in my framework – that managers view as important for personal and organizational success. I nevertheless want to justify the relevance of these four roles across all industries. By putting the case for including these four non-job roles in the performance framework, I'm not suggesting the other competencies mentioned are not relevant.

Two of the roles in the non-job roles framework are interpersonal and the other two are personal. We'll look at the four non-job roles in that light.

Interpersonal non-job roles

Let's start with the positive mental attitude and enthusiasm role. It is virtually impossible to be positive and enthusiastic all the time at work, or anywhere else for that matter. But equally, it would seem that being negative and lacking enthusiasm all the time is impossible – and undesirable – too. Although I have met some people that test this thesis! I am sure you would agree that people's attitude does affect those around them. And this is the main reason I have categorized it as an interpersonal non-job role; although it must be said that one's attitude is a personal choice.

I think it is reasonable to expect people to maintain – most of the time – a positive mental attitude and enthusiasm at work. It is, after all, the number one job competency identified in the top ten list of competencies we mentioned earlier. With the considerable pressures on organizations to constantly and rapidly "chop and change," being positive is necessary for building and maintaining high morale through these relentless adjustments and disruptions.

Employees are now expected to "do more with less" and this adds another layer of pressure. On top of all this, heightened competition, the increasing obsession in i-dotting and t-crossing discussed in Chapter 4, and the imposition of accountability and transparency regimes, elevate stress levels even further. Upholding a positive attitude and showing enthusiasm can be an antidote to these modern-day pressures and stresses; the need for cultivating a harmonious working environment is as important now as ever before. So it is unsurprising – with all these strains – that this competency is first on the list of most wanted job skills.

The second interpersonal non-job role in the framework is the team role. With the erosion of hierarchy and the corresponding flattening of organizational structures, teams are now the dominant organizing work structure. So being a "team player" is naturally a sought after competency in the contemporary workplace. Employees are being called upon to participate in short- and long-term project teams, often with people they have never meet, let alone worked with before. These cross-functional project teams are set up to deal with specific problems or issues, utilizing employees with a wide range of expertise and diversity of perspectives. Working harmoniously and constructively with others in these team structures is a core non-job competency.

We saw that the seventh most valued job competency was to be *able to work in a team*; managers recognize, understandably, that effectively cooperating with others is a vital skill. But being a team player is not as simple as it sounds; it is a complex combination of skills, knowledge, and attitudes. For instance, you need to have the capacity to influence and also be open to being influenced by your fellow team members; be able to juggle the dual accountabilities of individual and team outputs; be able to work cooperatively and harmoniously with others under duress; and be willing and able to interact and exchange information with a variety of stakeholders. Despite its complicatedness, the ability to work in team environments benefits organizations, managers, and employees.

Personal non-job roles

The first of the two personal non-job roles I will briefly define is the career development role. This role is about the employee continually growing and developing technically and personally. As with the other non-job roles, I don't think it is unreasonable to expect an employee to be a lifelong learner in their career; though we've all met people who have stopped learning and developing in their career by their own choosing. When challenged, these stagnant employees often give a lame excuse, such as: "I'm too old to learn anything new." Or when invited to expand their career skills-set, they retort with: "I'm just happy doing what I have always done." Having the desire to continually improve, upgrade, and expand their skill-base and develop personally benefits not only the employee, but their current and future employer.

AT THE COAL FACE...

The bane of automation

For several decades we have been repeatedly warned of the need to expand and diversify our repertoire of career skills. The looming threat – should we decide not to upgrade and diversify our skills-set – is a machine designed to replace us, or at least replace what we currently do in our work. It's called automation.

I observed first-hand an example of automation several years ago. Consulting to a horticulture business specializing in producing seedlings – I admit – I knew very little about plants, but do know a reasonable amount about people and their motivations.

Anyway, three employees in this seedling business lost their jobs overnight. For six months we (the owner and me) tried to convince these unskilled laborers to learn a new set of skills in other parts of the business. But they steadfastly refused. They explained that they were happy manually putting seeds into trays of soil, one-by-one, and over-and-over again, every day. Apart from being repetitious and boring, I could see a day when a machine could do this faster and less costly with the same level of quality. That day came faster than I thought. More significantly, it came faster than the three employees may have expected, or wanted.

One day they turned up for work to be confronted by a giant machine that did the job of ten people; this mechanical structure didn't want to be paid; you just plugged it into the wall! Regrettably these good employees – who had given great service to the seedling company – were shown the door. There was no other option available.

Referring back to the list of top ten competencies, the ninth most valuable job skill is a *willingness to learn*. This is defined as *the capacity to maintain a mind that is open to new ways of doing things and willing to accept constructive feedback*. To be able to continually grow and develop as an employee and person, people need an attitude of open-mindedness to new possibilities and a keenness to reflect on feedback. To illustrate my point, consider the closed-minded attitude and reluctance to accept feedback from the three employees in the case above.

There are two elements to the career development role. One element relates to technical-development. Basically this involves making career decisions about education, training, and career options. The second element is about self-development. This is really about developing oneself to assist in carrying out employment duties now and in the future. For instance, personal development can cover such things as effectively managing time and priorities, developing "people skills," minimizing stress, and so on. Exercising the career development role, like the other non-job roles, will have widespread benefits.

The final of the four non-job roles in the framework, and the second of the personal non-job roles, is the innovation and continuous improvement role. While the career development role is directed at improving the individual, the innovation and continuous improvement role is concerned with improving the organization.

This role is basically about offering constructive suggestions and changes in how the business functions. Innovation and continuous improvement covers a wide range of factors in the workplace. For instance, it may include improving the quality of products or service, reducing time and costs, increasing output and safety, meeting deadlines, enhancing interpersonal cooperation, or streamlining systems and processes. For organizations to survive and thrive in a climate of accelerated change and uncertainty, like employees, they need to be in a constant state of growth and development; employees have an important role to play in this regard.

Referring back to the list of top job competencies, the skill most closely aligned with this role is number three: *Self-motivation/initiative. Taking responsibility for originating tasks/new ideas/methods and the ability to think and act without being prompted* is an important precursor to innovation and continuous improvement. Getting people engaged in improving the organization they are employed by has been a perennial and frustrating challenge since Peter Senge introduced us to the concept of the *learning organization* over a quarter of a century ago; we discussed this in Chapter 2.

Under the old psychological contract, modernizing and improving the workplace was the sole province of the manager, not the employee. But under the new contract, there is a different expectation. The expectation is one where this responsibility for business improvement is shared between manager and employee.

Gaining an advantage over competitors is the ultimate driver for business success. Competitive advantage comes from being flexible and maneuverable in response to fluctuating conditions in the marketplace, such as newly implemented legislation or new trends. This agility doesn't come from "doing things like we always have"; it comes from questioning the *status quo* and being prepared to continually change the way things are done in all aspects of the business.

The benefits of the framework

It is hard to argue against the relevance these four non-job roles have on work performance. This two-dimensional non-job roles framework addresses several weaknesses in the conventional job performance framework. The new framework is multi-dimensional rather than one-dimensional, accounting for multiple roles employees may take on in the workplace. Because this framework accounts for multiple roles, it fills gaps associated with typical performance measures that only focus on the job role.

For instance, someone can be technically proficient, but not a team player. Or, these technically competent individuals may not add any value to their role, being disinclined to offer suggestions for continuous improvement in processes and systems, and lacking enterprise and initiative when needed. This same individual may be unwilling to develop their skills-set on the job. The roles of maintaining a positive mental attitude and enthusiasm, being a team player, growing and developing oneself technically and personally, and contributing to business improvement are widely and progressively more recognized as vital sub-dimensions of performance across all industries.

So this framework of non-job performance has a broader, more general application than traditional measures of performance, which are still in most cases too job-centric. The four non-job roles framework of performance can be applied to all industries, occupations, and jobs.

These organizational roles are outside the range of the typical job description. An employee who is prepared to perform these non-job roles in addition to completely satisfying the requirements of their job role, is accomplishing more than what is stated in their job description. By taking responsibility for these non-job roles, an employee is adding value to their employment. Briefly, this employee is displaying a greater commitment to the work they do than the position they hold.

In addition to their job role, an employee dedicated to performing these non-job roles is adopting a two-dimensional approach to performance at work. Such an employee holds a belief that what they do is more important than the position they hold. They understand that their contribution is greater than completing a defined bundle of job tasks competently. The employee's sense of identity, self-esteem, and purpose is not dependent exclusively on the position they occupy in the organizational chart.

When an individual allows their identity to wholly reside with their workplace position, they become organizationally-dependent; they become a captive of their job description. On the surface, the employer probably doesn't see this as problematic; to the contrary, it can be confused with demonstrating dedication. But this way of thinking is a predicament. This mindset can lock an employee into a permanent victim relationship, perpetually subservient to the organization. This can inhibit the contextual performance of non-job work.

For instance, it is unlikely that an employee beholden to the literal limits of a job description, will readily exhibit cross-functional teamwork, if it potentially interferes with their task-related KPIs. This same employee – captive to their job description – will be less inclined to explore and undertake personal development opportunities not specific to the demands of their current job. An organizationally-dependent employee is more likely to faithfully comply with standard operating procedures than being constructively critical of the business's systems and practices. The idea of performing for this employee is tied up first and foremost with doing their "job" to the best of their ability.

These four non-job roles are in high demand; we can see this from the research. Promoting the performance of the competencies associated with these non-job roles is beneficial to the employee career-wise, and the workplace they are applied in. Managers evidently want to attract and retain people who exhibit these skills and behaviors. Employees too, are better served viewing their array of skills and work identity as transferable and independent of any one organizational position or setting. Being shackled psychologically to the specifications of a job is not ultimately useful to either that job-holder or their employer.

It is paradoxically helpful for organizations to be populated with an autonomous-thinking workforce. Managers need to be able to reap the benefits of free-thinking and unrestrained contributors. For instance, an independently-minded employee will appreciate the need to develop their skills-set in the interests of their career. Employees who are not prisoners confined to the psychological constraints of a tightly controlled job specification, are much more likely – as I mentioned – to constructively question established approaches and practices. This same employee may then offer alternative ways of doing things that may be better, faster, or easier. Led well, a self-regulating worker can be an asset to any business by not being too emotionally tied up to their job-post.

Benefits, status symbols, and policies that favor tenure over performance, and internal pleasing over customer service, are symptomatic of a job-focus, not a performance-focus. As I said in *The 8 Values of Highly Productive Companies: Creating Wealth from a New Employment Relationship*:

> If the company's efforts are in any way distracted from doing quality work in the service of customers, it diminishes overall performance. Independent and performance-focused employees who look outward toward their customers are increasingly in greater demand by companies. These independently-minded employees are the key to a robust commercial future.[3]

Work performance begins with changing the focus from remunerating employees on the basis of time spent on the job to remuneration based on the achievement of KPIs. These KPIs should cover both job and non-job roles we have covered in this chapter. The old saying: "A fair day's work for a fair day's pay" is a mindset suited to the 20th century, not the 21st century. The next four chapters are each devoted to the four non-job roles mentioned here in this introductory chapter for Part II. Specifically, it is my intention to define each role, consider the key elements of that particular role, and identify the critical KPIs.

In Chapter 6, we start with the positive mental attitude and enthusiasm role.

The **Top 10** Key Points …

 The work that employees engage in is two-dimensional. The job description documents one of these two dimensions: The technical or task-related dimension.

2. The transformative changes in the workplace since the mid-1980s have brought into question work performance and what it does and doesn't involve.

3. A role description adds another dimension; it includes the non-job dimension in addition to the job dimension of work.

4. With the role description, the employee has five roles to perform: One job role and four non-job roles.

5. There's a plethora of terms and processes used around the world to capture the essence of what someone does at work. But overall, the document itself is commonly referred to as a job or position description.

6. From an organization development perspective, the non-job roles the employee performs well, not too well, or poorly can be as impactful to the performance of an enterprise as the execution of job-tasks.

7. The role description consists of five roles – one job role and four non-job roles.

8. Contextual performance covers multiple sub-dimensions of work, such as attitude and enthusiasm, teamwork, growth and development, and innovation and continuous improvement.

9. The non-job roles framework consists of positive mental attitude and enthusiasm; team; career development; and innovation and continuous improvement roles.

10. Benefits, status symbols, and policies that favor tenure over performance, and internal pleasing over customer service, are symptomatic of a job-focus, not a performance-focus.

6

The Positive Mental Attitude and Enthusiasm Role

What of the person who gets the technical requirements of their job done to a high standard but is, nevertheless, toxic to deal with and be around? Is this acceptable? If an employee is always moaning and bitching and belly-aching, should this be excusable on the basis that they are performing the tasks in their job description?

John is a highly skilled and experienced accountant. He has worked on many complex financial projects throughout his career in five countries. John is particularly good at addressing the needs of clients. He knows how to turn their concepts into tangible and viable financial structures. But John has a major problem.

Although technically great at his job, John is extremely difficult to work with. He has a short temper and is often disrespectful; often coming across to others in the office as arrogant. John "doesn't suffer fools gladly." He dominates team meetings; everyone else is too afraid to speak. And those team members who are brave enough to speak – particularly when they disagree with John – are often ridiculed. If these same team members persist in pushing their point, John will often shout them down.

On a couple of occasions, these confrontations have almost come to physical blows. Several junior accountants have left and gone to work for the opposition accounting firms. This situation can't continue; something has to change.

John's manager has a dilemma on his hands. Does he put up with the interpersonal shortcomings on the basis that John has outstanding skills as a senior accountant? Does he put John on notice that unless he learns to be easier to deal with, he will be "shown the door"? Or does he "bite the bullet" and let him go, knowing that the firm's competition will undoubtedly snap him up, along with his impressive client base? What to do?

There are myriad clichés, quotes, and sayings about the advantages of possessing a positive mental attitude and displaying enthusiasm. I don't want to regurgitate these statements in this chapter; they are everywhere we care to look. This is undoubtedly because a positive attitude and enthusiasm are important traits in the workplace; we value this quality in others.

This is not a self-help book. But needless to say, having an optimistic attitude and showing enthusiasm for the work being undertaken is advantageous for all concerned. In fact, in the list of top ten job competencies we looked at in the previous chapter it is considered the number one valued competency. Other surveys back up the relevance of this competency in the workplace. This is largely why it is one of the four roles in the non-job roles framework.

A positive attitude and an enthusiastic approach to work are of great personal consequence to the person exhibiting this competency. After all, most of us spend at least a third of our working lives at work. Just to put that into perspective, this amounts to 40 years at 46 weeks a year or 230 days of approximately eight hours a day. All up, this amounts to 73,600 hours at work in the lifetime of an employee. That is a long time to choose to be negative and apathetic. One would think that due to the long time we spend at work in our lifetime – at the very least – showing up at work reasonably happy and wholehearted most of the time is a logical conclusion. It is surprising, nonetheless, how many people don't seem to want to do this. It doesn't make any sense!

Apart from gaining at least some semblance of joy from their work, the right attitude and enthusiasm is important in our dealings with other people. What about the people who we work closely with? Do our attitude and levels of interest affect those we work side-by-side with? Having a positive or negative way of thinking and being passionate or apathetic undoubtedly has a significant bearing on others. Some people may dispute this. But we have all experienced working with people who either have a positive or negative approach to their work and we know how this influences us.

We all know instinctively that a person's attitude rubs off on other people. For instance, it can often only take one person with a rotten attitude to pollute a team of six to eight employees. The opposite is true too: A person with a positive attitude can energize others in the team. For this reason, I think employees ought to take responsibility for the attitude they bring to work. Let me qualify this claim: I am not suggesting that an employee is expected to come to work every day "bouncing off the walls" and brimming with unbridled excitement and passion. A person with a positive mental attitude and enthusiasm in the workplace is someone, in my view, who is solution-focused not problem-focused; they have the attitude of wanting to solve a problem rather than complaining about it. It is an employee who willingly takes on the tasks that need doing without their boss standing over them with a big stick. Put simply, this employee takes on the tasks they are responsible for completing with a general attitude of positivity and enthusiasm.

Team members exhibiting a positive approach to their work actively try to elevate the mood of the team they belong to, not sabotage it. This team member is willing to have a go without complaining and whining about everything and everybody. We are all capable of demonstrating these characteristics, despite the fact that many don't.

To behave in this way is habitual. It is a choice; a decision. We can decide the attitude we want to bring to work, or anywhere else for that matter. Any employee can choose to have a consistently positive attitude and exhibit enthusiasm. They can also choose – and unfortunately many do – to be relentlessly negative and destructive and parade apathy toward the work that needs to be done.

By acknowledging a positive mental attitude and enthusiasm as a significant non-job role, we are openly setting a standard and demonstrating a belief that people ought to show up at work in this way. And if organizations are prepared to make a statement that this is one of the non-job roles that employees are expected to play in the workplace, we will certainly see more, not less, of this sought-after behavior.

Why shouldn't it be a requirement of all employees to demonstrate this non-job competency, and behave accordingly? We know that not all employees demonstrate a good attitude and high level of enthusiasm. But could it be due to this behavior characteristic not being stated as an expected role of the employee at work? We know it is highly valued, but we also know that it is rarely elevated to the same status as the task-related competencies embedded in the job description.

Referring back to the competencies study mentioned in the previous chapter, *the ability to remain consistently positive and optimistic and to maintain enthusiasm in all work tasks and projects* was considered the most sought after job skill. We therefore unquestionably value this non-job competency highly. It is time we legitimized it as a significant part in the repertoire of successful employment requirements.

What of the person who gets the technical requirements of their job done to a high standard but is, nevertheless, toxic to deal with and be around? Is this acceptable? If an employee is always moaning and bitching and belly-aching, should this be excusable on the basis that they are performing the tasks in their job description? I guess the answer to these questions depends on the extent to which they are difficult to work with, on the one hand, and how good they are at their job-related tasks, on the other. But that negative attitude – to whatever degree it exists – is likely to adversely affect those who work in close proximity with that person. The negative attitude and apathetic demeanor of this technically proficient employee will almost certainly lessen team morale somehow and somewhat.

Although difficult to quantify, we know intuitively an unenthusiastic attitude is costly to the holder and those they interact with. And so it is on this basis alone that it is fair and reasonable to expect employees not to pollute their team with negativity, notwithstanding their technical know-how. By exhibiting a noxious attitude, or showing apathy, an employee is not fulfilling one of several important non-job roles.

So what specifically are the characteristics of this positive mental attitude and enthusiasm non-job role? These are the three core elements of the positive mental attitude and enthusiasm competency:

- Solution-focus.
- Taking responsibility.
- Positive energy.

When exercised together, this non-job role can be a powerful contributor to workplace performance. But it is true that these traits are not universally exercised across all industries by all employees. Furthermore, we all interpret these characteristics differently. What is beyond doubt, though, is that an employee exhibiting a positive mental attitude and enthusiasm is going to be an asset to any team, department, or organization.

But how do we measure these elements? What are the key indicators? The fact that a positive mental attitude and enthusiasm can be interpreted differently in so many situations and contexts means that identifying some KPIs is important. Although it is impossible to measure this role objectively, it is possible to set some universal indicators and mutually agreed upon expectations between manager and employee.

Expectations can be arrived at through dialogue and discussion, and informed by critical incidents in the workplace. I'll spend more time in Part III suggesting a methodology for "measuring" this and the other three non-job roles.

In the meantime, I shall define these three elements of the positive mental attitude and enthusiasm role.

Solution-focus

Having a *solution-focus* basically means this: To look for answers to problems. It doesn't mean concentrating attention on the problem itself. In other words, being solution-focused is being prepared to explore possibilities for resolving workplace dilemmas. To be able to apply this readiness means considering alternative solutions and exercising appropriate initiative and enterprise, either on one's own, or as part of a team. In very practical terms, it involves considering and implementing solutions or options before simply "passing the buck."

Being solution-focused begins with this question: "How can this problem be resolved?" Not: "Why is this happening to me?" or "How can I pass the responsibility for fixing this onto someone else, such as my manager?" This doesn't mean a solution-focused employee resolves all issues and problems on their own, without the assistance of their colleagues. But it does mean that when a solution-focused employee has to involve others in the problem-solving process, they have at least thought through possible solutions and resolutions. By being focused on the solution, the employee's colleagues, by the time they are involved in the problem-solving process, have a potential starting point rather than beginning from scratch.

Take, for example, a customer who calls a computer retail business and asks for some repair work to be done on their computer. Henry – the employee – books the computer in for repair on the assumption that it still falls within the warranty period and that the repairs would therefore be free-of-charge. After getting off the phone to the customer, he discovers that the warranty period lapsed two days before the repair job was logged. What to do? The customer is expecting her computer will be repaired at no cost. If Henry didn't have a solution-focused attitude he would just explain this situation to his manager and wait for the manager to come up with a solution.

But Henry considers an array of possible solutions. Henry considers one possibility might be to complete the work free-of-charge to maintain goodwill with this customer. He notes that this is the third computer she has purchased from the business. Another possibility Henry considers is to suggest that the customer pay half the cost of repair, as an acknowledgement of their good custom but also recognizing that the repair work is outside the warranty period. Neither of these potential solutions is described in the business policy and procedures manual. Either way, Henry has offered his boss two possible solutions for further consideration.

Table 6.1 illustrates the KPIs for the first of the three elements of the positive mental attitude and enthusiasm competency: Solution-focus.

Before discussing the related competencies for these KPIs, I'd like to point out several uniform features of Table 6.1 that apply to all subsequent KPI tables. The following three chapters contain tables with the same format. First, each of these tables lists ten KPIs. These KPIs are shown in the column on the left-hand side of the table. Why ten? Apart from being a round figure, ten KPIs are enough indicators to gauge whether or not an employee is consistently exhibiting that element of the non-job role. It also means that more than one competency associated with the element of the non-job role can be scrutinized.

The second key feature you will notice from the table is that the KPIs are written in the first person. As an important part of the process of evaluating these KPIs, each employee will assess themselves in conjunction with two other workplace perspectives. I am also suggesting that the employee's manager and several observers should have input into this process too. I will have more to say about this in Chapter 11.

And the third feature of the table that I think is important to mention is the rating scale on the far right-hand side. You will observe that it is scaled from five to one, in terms of agreement with each statement. In this case:

- *Five* means I strongly agree.
- *Four* means I agree.

TABLE 6.1 KPIs for Solution-focus

Element: Solution-focus					
Key performance indicators	5	4	3	2	1
1. When encountering an uncommon problem in my work, my first reaction is to consider some ways of resolving it.					
2. When a situation calls for a new approach, I consider ways of resolving workplace dilemmas that are not standard operating procedures.					
3. I am prepared to investigate a range of solutions for fixing problems at work.					
4. I show initiative when faced with a problem at work that doesn't necessarily have a straightforward answer.					
5. I am prepared to work with others in a constructive and collaborative manner to resolve workplace dilemmas.					
6. I am "solution-focused" rather than "problem-focused."					
7. When asked by my manager for a solution to a complex problem in my work area, I have usually thought this through.					
8. I see it as my responsibility to come up with multiple ways of resolving challenging problems affecting my work.					
9. When others offer suggestions for solving problems, I am generally open to considering them in the first instance.					
10. I consider myself a good problem-solver.					

- *Three* means I neither agree nor disagree.
- *Two* means I disagree.
- *One* means I strongly disagree.

It is useful to bear in mind these three points when reading all the subsequent tables in Part II. Returning specifically to the KPIs in Table 6.1, relating to the element of solution-focus, there are three non-job competencies relating to the statements. First, there is a competency of *preparedness to use a variety of approaches and ideas to problem-solve.* Second, there is a competency of an employee's *willingness to work with others in solving problems.* Third, some KPIs consider the competency of *interacting effectively with their manager* with regard to problem-solving. Solution-focus is the first of three elements of the non-job role of positive mental attitude and enthusiasm.

Taking responsibility

Taking responsibility implies not shirking a duty. It means taking on tasks willingly without first being told to do so by others. By taking responsibility, the employee demonstrates self-reliance; they complete their responsibilities without being prompted. What's more, an employee with this trait is going to initiate tasks, advance new ideas, devise methods, and think and act without being pressed by their manager. Taking responsibility also entails working constructively with others to get projects done. Apportioning blame and making excuses is the antithesis of a "taking responsibility" attitude.

An employee who is keen to take responsibility actively seeks out opportunities to exercise their initiative beyond the scope of their job description. They will offer assistance to others when needed, they look for chances to help others, they show empathy, offer suggestions, and are constructive.

For example, Marcia voluntarily stays late after closing time one evening. She has a report to finish for her boss, Sam. Sam has asked for this report some time tomorrow, but Marcia has a whole host of jobs to do the next day that need her attention. So, without any pressure from her boss, she works late, without complaint or martyrdom, and completes the report. And before shutting down, turning off the light, and turning on the security sensors, Marcia sends the report to Sam's inbox and away she goes.

TABLE 6.2   KPIs for Taking responsibility

Element: Taking responsibility					
Key performance indicators	5	4	3	2	1
1. I usually complete tasks on time and to a high standard.					
2. I take the initiative and complete tasks without being asked to do so.					
3. I have a reputation for generating fresh ideas and alternative ways of getting things done in the workplace.					
4. I would describe myself as a self-starter.					
5. I see it as my responsibility to get my work done on time and to a high standard.					
6. I always try to work in a cooperative manner with those around me.					
7. I don't apportion blame and make excuses when things go wrong.					
8. I take complete ownership and responsibility for the work that needs doing.					
9. When given a task to do, I can be relied upon to get it done.					
10. I consider myself to be fairly resourceful when I need to be.					

Table 6.2 illustrates the KPIs for the second element of the role of positive mental attitude and enthusiasm: Taking responsibility.

The ten KPIs associated with taking responsibility in Table 6.2 are centered on three non-job competencies. Some of the KPIs are related to the competency of *taking responsibility for getting work done on time and of a high standard*. The second competency relates to *working with others in a cooperative fashion*. Finally, the remaining statements revolve around the competency of *resourcefulness and showing initiative*. These KPIs describe the element of taking responsibility, the second characteristic of the positive mental attitude and enthusiasm non-job role.

Enterprising behavior at the enterprise

A small firm of marketing consultants is going through a rough patch and needs to cut their business overheads. Sue-Ellen, the owner of the business, tells her staff of eight that she wants them to put forward cost-cutting ideas. She points out to them all in a meeting that this does not include making anyone redundant and further, if the ideas are good, this may secure their jobs in the future.

Subsequently, she receives several suggestions privately and decides it is time to call another meeting of all eight to discuss these ideas in details. If any of these ideas have merit, Sue-Ellen will implement them in her business immediately, or at some convenient time in the future.

However, the meeting quickly descends into an unstructured rabble; everyone is trying to explain the virtues of their own ideas. Nobody is really listening to anybody else's ideas. Little progress is being made. The meeting falls into suggestions, counter-suggestions, and argument and counter-argument as to who has the best idea. If it wasn't so serious, it would be hilarious to watch.

Helen, one of the junior marketing consultants, has a well thought through cost-cutting measure. Her proposal is to pur-chase a data projector and screen for the numerous marketing campaigns and proposals the firm makes to its clients. The cur-rent arrangement is that this equipment is hired on an hourly basis when required.

Although young and somewhat inexperienced, Helen has a great reputation as a hard and trusted worker in the firm, and as such, she has considerable respect with her colleagues.

In preparation for the meeting, Helen has researched some figures to back up her case for purchasing the equipment. She investigated the cost of purchasing the data projector and screen and compared this cost to the costs of hiring the same equip-ment over the last 18 months of her employment with the firm.

She waits for a quiet moment in the meeting before putting her case forward. Based on her research, Helen strongly argues that it would save the business a hefty amount if they invested in the new equipment. She makes a convincing case, supporting her idea with figures. Helen has gathered evidence and assertively communicates her plan to the rest of the team with the confidence that comes from having done her homework thoroughly.

One of her colleagues challenges her. The colleague's counter argument is that one of the reasons for hiring the equipment in the first place was that any technical hitches or breakdowns were covered and that a technician would arrive on site within 20 minutes to fix the problem or alternatively, replace the data projector.

She has anticipated this objection to her plan and counters this argument surely and convincingly. Helen points out that she has specifically asked the company they would buy the equipment from what would happen in the circumstance of a breakdown or malfunction. She points out that the company selling the product has an on-site technician who would travel to the destination and fix the problem immediately, free-of-charge.

Sue-Ellen is impressed and persuaded by Helen's idea and the fact that it is backed up by figures. She asks Helen to go ahead and order the data projector and screen. Sue-Ellen is in awe of the young marketing consultant and her proactive and responsible approach to the business's financial position.

Also, Sue-Ellen makes a mental note to involve Helen in the company's future purchasing decisions.[1]

Positive energy

Positive energy is engaging with fellow employees with an optimistic frame-of-mind. It means contributing to conversations and team meetings in a constructive manner. In interacting with others, an employee exhibiting positive energy is cheerful, respectful, and polite. Positive energy also means being approachable and engaging and not inaccessible and despondent.

The attitude necessary for possessing positive energy is being grateful and happy to be part of the team. It means too, appreciating the efforts of others. In sum, displaying positive energy comes from having a general enthusiasm about the work that needs to be done and a gratefulness for the efforts of others.

It is an enjoyable experience working alongside someone who demonstrates positive energy; they are "low maintenance" and good company; they energize their colleagues. At a basic level, employees with this attitude understand that they have an obligation to be as optimistic as possible; they ought to be constructive in the interests of the smooth functioning of the team. In short, they are enjoyable and engaging colleagues to be around at work.

As an illustration of what I mean by positive energy, Samantha was involved in a team meeting that was descending into a downward spiral of negativity. Everyone was blaming everybody else, from the CEO to the janitor, for their woes. Samantha decided it was best to not "add fuel to the fire." She was sensitive and aware of her contributions to the team meeting. Samantha tactfully pointed out some of the "wins" the team had achieved lately and how she enjoyed being associated with those successes. She empathized with the frustrations of her team. But Samantha was also positive and upbeat and injected a different perspective into the conversation. Her attitude helped to change the negative tenor of the meeting.

Table 6.3 illustrates the KPIs for the third element of the role of positive mental attitude and enthusiasm: Positive energy.

These ten KPIs in Table 6.3 are based on two competencies. The first competency is to be able to *create positive interpersonal encounters with colleagues*. And the other indicators relate to the competency of employee's ability to contribute to *cultivating a positive working environment*. The

TABLE 6.3   **KPIs for Positive energy**

Element: Positive energy					
Key performance indicators	5	4	3	2	1
1. In most workplace situations, I am positive and constructive.					
2. I always try to be empathetic to the needs of others around me.					
3. I show respect for the views and perspectives of my colleagues, even when I don't necessarily agree with them.					
4. People usually find me very approachable.					
5. People would consider me a positive person.					
6. I am appreciative of my job and the work I do in this organization.					
7. People generally find me a "breath of fresh air" to work with.					
8. I make an effort to have good working relationships with everyone I come into contact with at work.					
9. I generally go about my work with positivity.					
10. In the work environment, I have the capacity to put myself in the shoes of other people, and do so regularly.					

KPIs are associated with the element of positive energy, the third and final characteristic of the positive mental attitude and enthusiasm non-job role.

I have defined what I mean by positive mental attitude and enthusiasm and mounted an argument for why it is a significant non-job role for an employee. The role has been broken down into three elements. In summary, the three elements are: Solution-focus, taking responsibility, and positive energy. The three tables in this chapter cover 30 KPIs that are related to several competencies. These are the guideposts to determine whether the employee is fulfilling this role in their work.

In the next chapter, we look at the second of two interpersonal non-job roles: Being a team player.

The **Top 10** Key Points …

1. Apart from gaining at least some semblance of joy from our work, the right attitude and enthusiasm is important in our dealings with other people.

2. By acknowledging a positive mental attitude and enthusiasm as a significant non-job role, we are openly setting a standard and demonstrating a belief that people ought to show up at work in this way.

3. These are the three core elements of the positive mental attitude and enthusiasm competency: Solution-focus, taking responsibility, and positive energy.

4. Having a solution-focus means looking for answers to problems more willingly than concentrating attention on the problem itself.

5. There are three competencies supporting the element of solution-focus: Preparedness to use a variety of approaches and ideas to problem-solve; willingness to work with others in solving problems; and interacting effectively with their manager with regard to problem-solving.

6. The second element of the positive mental attitude and enthusiasm role is taking responsibility, implying not shirking a duty. It means taking on tasks willingly without first being told to do so by others.

7. There are three competencies supporting the element of taking responsibility: Taking responsibility for getting work done on time and of a high standard; working with others in a cooperative fashion; and resourcefulness and showing initiative.

8. The third element of the positive mental attitude and enthusiasm role is positive energy. It means engaging with fellow employees with an optimistic frame-of-mind, including contributing to conversations and team meetings in a constructive manner.

9. There are two competencies for the element positive energy: Create positive interpersonal encounters with colleagues and cultivating a positive working environment.

10. The three tables in this chapter cover 30 KPIs that are related to the elements and competencies of this non-job role. These are the indicators to determine whether the employee is fulfilling this role in their work.

chapter 7

The Team Role

Working and functioning in teams or tribes is as old as civilization itself. It is hardwired into us as a survival instinct.

The newly appointed CEO Melissa identified her first major hurdle as one of breaking down the boundaries between departments in the government agency she now leads. She had observed that the agency – like most government departments – is organized around several "silos." From Melissa's early observations, this organization is predominantly structured around functions. This is particularly evident at the senior management level. The team that ought to be the least divided and most cross-functionally focused – the senior management – is disjoined and doesn't operate as a team.

Melissa witnessed managers arriving at executive meetings with their functional "hat" on and consequently unable to consider issues from the perspective of the overall organization. She knew she had her work cut out in breaking down these deeply entrenched departmental boundaries.

She observed that the level of cooperation between these departments was minimal, even non-existent in some cases. Melissa was determined to change this. She reviewed the organizational structure, which was based on hierarchy and segmented across several functions.

Melissa decided to instigate several cross-functional project teams. She illustrated these teams in the organizational chart to highlight their prominence. For example, one team was formulated to look at ways of improving communication across the organization. Representatives were selected from all departments. Another cross-functional project team was set up to review systems and processes. And others too were put in place by the new CEO.

Peter was invited from the marketing department to serve on one of these project teams by the CEO. He seemed quite excited about being chosen, recognizing the need to improve cross-functional communication within the organization. Peter was approached directly by Melissa. He went to talk to the marketing manager in her office. Mary was less than enthusiastic when Peter told her about this development.

"I wish the CEO had spoken to me first," Mary protested, a little frustrated. "I can't afford to release you to attend these 'talk fests.' Peter, you are too valuable to the department. We are already short staffed. How often does she want you to attend these meetings?"

"I don't know," replied Peter a little deflated. "She hasn't told me."

"Well, it sounds like a complete waste of time. Your primary responsibility according to your job description is with my department, Peter," said Mary firmly. "You are a critical person to this department, and I'll have to speak to the CEO about this and let her know my feelings."

Peter left Mary's office disheartened and confused. He had thought that this was a great opportunity to break down the silos in the organization and improve communication across the agency. He couldn't understand his boss's reaction.[1]

Organizations structured around hierarchies have served us well for over a century. The principle characteristics of this formal structure – stability and clarity – were the core strengths. But now they are liabilities. The functionally-based organizing structure is inflexible and slow to respond to marketplace deviations that are characteristically sharp and sudden. As an organizing structure, the hierarchy is entirely unsuitable in the climate we are confronted with.

More specifically, organizations structured around divisions, departments, units, branches, or sections are less receptive to constant, sudden, and erratic fluctuations in external market forces and conditions. The hierarchy was, however, suitable for the 20th century, with its comparatively steady and predictable marketplace. But the enterprise structured around functions is unsuitable in today's fast-paced and volatile marketplace. Vertical channels of communication, supported by a clearly defined chain-of-command, prove sluggish when rapid response time is paramount.

So it is unsurprising, given the changing marketplace we work in, that cross-functional communication is becoming the dominant mode of communication. The vertical chain-of-command is giving way to lateral forms of communication. Most activity in the workplace needs timely input from several sources scattered far and wide across the business; not to mention outside the business too. So the dominant organizing structure is fast becoming the cross-functional temporary or permanent project team.

These changes in structure and communication require the employee to participate in teams "outside" their functional area; this is now an important part of their work. Work processing has changed dramatically from being fragmented across organizational boundaries in small, separated, bite-size pieces to large-scale, integrated multi-disciplinary teams.

This profound change in the way people work brings into question the continued reliance on the job description. The job description is designed around the work of an individual employee; it is based on segmenting rather than integrating work processing.

But the conventional thinking of work specialization is still prevalent. The reliance on the job description perpetuates this outdated thinking. For instance, the well intentioned employee naturally articulates this obsolete mindset along the lines of "I have a job to do and my job is to do this work as specified in my job description." This is despite the new reality of work processing that we face. The new reality can be expressed more accurately by an employee along the lines of: "In collaboration with several teams, I have a number of roles to play in getting the organizational work done right and on time." These teams are now made up of many permutations and combinations, depending upon the project or task that needs to be done.

Individual performance versus team performance

Temporary teams are formed around specific problems, projects, and tasks rather than specific disciplines, functions, or specializations. Notwithstanding this changing work landscape, the functional mindset still pervades the psyche of the manager and employee. This 20th-century outlook is unquestionably enabled by the omnipotent job description.

In the meantime, teamwork, in its various forms, continues to be a critical factor in organizational performance. Working and functioning in teams or tribes is as old as civilization itself. It is hardwired into us as a survival instinct. The transformation from organizing around formal functional structures to informal cross-functional networks is here to stay for the foreseeable future. This is in spite of our thinking still catching up.

In the traditional employment relationship model I illustrated in Chapter 4, one of the eight shared values is functional-based work. As such, the conventional-thinking employee's work identity is linked to their unit, department, and division first and foremost. In the new employment relationship model discussed in Chapter 5, functional-based work is replaced by a completely different shared value: Project-based work. Employees have always worked in teams. But in the past – and in many cases now – they were homogeneous, functional teams. In the new contract, employees are expected to work in several teams in a variety of contexts with many people from varied backgrounds and specialties. Although this move has been in progress for some time, performance rewards and recognition are still predominantly based on individual accomplishment.

Properly thought through and instituted gain-sharing plans and team-based incentives encourage suitable team behaviors; they reinforce the relevance of teamwork and its link to performance. However, we are sending mixed signals to employees. On the one hand, we make it clear that team work is a highly desirable behavior. On the other hand, we remunerate and reward people on the basis of their individual contribution. This confuses the employee.

As a good illustration of this contradiction, I was invited to help build better team work in a chain of retail travel agencies several years ago. I vividly recall standing in one of the typically busy retail travel agency outlets, discussing the topic of team performance with the owner of the business. I asked him to describe a usual incident that illustrated a lack of team work. The managing director without hesitation told me a story of an episode that occurred during a travel agent's well-earned lunch break. On the absent travel agent's desk was a phone message to follow-up the sale of an international flight. The lunch-bound travel agent decided to deal with this later. While he was out of the office, a member of his "team" decided to take the message from his desk and return the customer's call. This travel agent politely indicated to the customer that his colleague was "busy" and that under these circumstances, could he arrange the flights and payment for him? The answer from the customer was affirmative.

I interrupted the owner's story at this point and asked him what was wrong with that behavior, thinking that it sounded like the epitome of good team work. In response to my question, the owner pointed out how the bonus system worked in his business. This put into perspective the behavior of the employee. At the end of each month, all the revenues generated by the individual agents are tallied up and put on a "leader board" for all staff to see in the back office of all retail outlets. The larger the revenue generated by the agent in the month, the greater the bonus. This naturally generated huge incentive (and pressure) for each individual agent to sell as many airline tickets as possible during the month.

So the travel agent "following-up" the message on his colleague's desk was doing this out of self-interest; it was an act of sabotage, not team work! At any rate, the customer was happy. I pointed out what seemed obvious to me to the owner; that is, the bonus system was the main impediment to team work. Further, until he changed the way he rewarded his staff, he couldn't realistically expect a change in behavior.

Notwithstanding the rhetoric around the value of teamwork, the predominant basis for pay-for-performance still continues to be individual performance; although this is gradually changing. Performance systems need to consider the contribution of appropriate team behavior in organizational performance. But this sounds easier than it is. As we discussed in Chapter 2, individualized reward systems are inexorably tied to the KPIs in the job description.

The job description mitigates team work. Job descriptions, as we have discussed, are vehicles to splinter the work of an organization into parts referred to as a *job*; this consequently individualizes work performance. The job analysis describes as precisely as possible what the individual job-holder is required to do to fulfill their work obligation. Each employee has their own job description. In the vast majority of organizations there isn't a corresponding and overarching document that describes in detail the interdependencies between jobs.

The lack of attention creates confusion in the mind of the employee. There is a general belief that the employee is supposed to work harmoniously and productively with their work colleagues within and outside their immediate team. But at the same time, the employee is issued with a job description that tells them what success looks like; that is, competing the literal requirements of the job description. The document breaks down the component parts of the job into small, measurable, bite-size pieces. This will – at times – put the employee in a dilemma. There can be conflict between attending to their KRAs and also exhibiting exemplary team behavior.

Furthermore, knowing recognition and rewards are usually linked to the KPIs in the job description, the employee is naturally drawn to the demands of their job. Demonstrating teamwork can "take a back seat"; it becomes a secondary consideration. For instance, an employee, who is under pressure to complete several transactions by month's end (part of their KPIs), is asked by another team to assist them to complete their transactions before month's end. What to do? Given a choice, this employee – probably with their boss's consent – will probably undertake the work specified in their job description. Undoubtedly, helping out a colleague and completing your own job tasks are both important in terms of performance. But the task-focus of the job description can make it easier and permissible to attend to matters that are counter to team work.

Several of the ten most valued job competencies we saw in Chapter 5 are characteristic of good teamwork. The most obvious one was stated as *able to work in a team*. But others are traits of being a team player too. For example, good communication skills are important when working collaboratively with others, particularly in a team environment. Being honest and liking people helps a lot too when working in a team environment. Being dependable and hardworking is also important. Similar to the other three non-job roles, functioning effectively in a team is an innate quality; anyone can learn this skill, or any of the other roles for that matter. You don't need some special inborn attribute to be good at working in teams. Although it is true that some are better than others, everyone can do this with a little help and encouragement.

So what specifically are the elements of the team role?

I have identified four elements that make up the team role competency. They are:

- Leadership.
- Accountability.
- Collaboration.
- Communication.

Let's consider each element in more detail.

Leadership

Showing *leadership* in teams means influencing others in a positive way, when the need arises. Working in teams by definition is a collaborative exercise. This involves sharing the leadership responsibilities of the team from time-to-time. Leading with influence could, for example, be asking a timely and thought-provoking question, offering a constructive suggestion, seeking clarification, or building consensus. Team leadership can also involve taking some ownership in improving processes, outcomes, and efficiencies. Being involved and engaged in team meetings and adopting a solution-focused attitude is part of the element of leadership. At its most basic level, team leadership is about exercising a constructive role in the deliberations of the team.

Showing leadership in teams also means showing a willingness to be persuaded by the views of other team members. This entails a preparedness to actively listen and constructively engage in dialogue and being open to considering alternative points-of-view expressed by colleagues. The corollary of this is being dogmatic and adopting fixed views, regardless of the arguments advanced by others. As the old cliché goes: "To lead, one must first be prepared to follow."

Let me illustrate leadership in a team context. Greg, one of the less vocal members of Brenda's team, is a member on the company's health and safety committee, a permanent cross-functional team. At the latest meeting, Greg decides to raise the matter of a set of stairs leading to the production area. He thinks the condition of the stairs may be a potential hazard. Brenda, who is chairing the meeting, bypasses the comment and moves swiftly onto the next agenda item so that she can complete the meeting on time. Jackie – a team colleague of Greg's – notices this and firmly and courteously says, "Excuse me Brenda; I would be interested in hearing what Greg has to say about those stairs, particularly if they are potentially dangerous." Brenda, apologizing to Greg, invites him to elaborate. Greg in his understated manner points out that the grip at the bottom of the stairs is starting to wear. He points out that this stairway, being a well-used thoroughfare between administration and production is potentially a safety hazard. Greg makes a valid point and the committee is obliged to acknowledge this as a subject for further investigation. Jackie demonstrated leadership by ensuring that Greg's voice was heard.

Table 7.1 illustrates the KPIs for the first of the four elements of the team role: Leadership.

The ten KPIs in Table 7.1 are based on three competencies. Success in some KPIs is supported by the ability to *influence or persuade others* in the team. Conversely, another competency is based on the capacity to be *flexible and open to the ideas of others* in the team. And finally, the remaining KPIs are based on the competency of a team member *appreciating their team role* as a positive and active contributor. These

TABLE 7.1 KPIs for Leadership

Element: Leadership					
Key performance indicators	5	4	3	2	1
1. People I work closely with respect my opinions.					
2. I can occasionally persuade my fellow team members on work-related matters.					
3. I am always an active and constructive contributor in team meetings.					
4. I am open to being persuaded by other team members, based on a good argument, from time-to-time.					
5. I contribute my fair share to the teams I belong to.					
6. I am comfortable taking the lead in my team when I have something important to contribute.					
7. I would consider myself a very active member of the teams I work in.					
8. When I disagree with a decision made by the majority of my team I accept this decision and move on easily.					
9. If I believe something can be done better, faster, or with less resources, I will speak up at team meetings and put my case.					
10. I enjoy making constructive contributions to my team colleagues from time-to-time.					

KPIs describe leadership in the context of the team role, the first of four characteristics of this non-job role.

Accountability

Accountability in this sense means accepting the dual responsibility for the work of the team the employee belongs to and their own individual work. This attitude takes into account an understanding of the impact of the work an employee does for their work unit, function, and organization. A person demonstrating this type of accountability doesn't see their work as isolated from the rest of the organization. They understand that the work they do affects the work of others and *vice versa*. Being responsible for ensuring that their work is done in a timely and effective manner is the hallmark of a team member who is prepared to be accountable.

Apart from appreciating the interdependencies in the workplace, an employee who is accountable also is prepared – strangely enough – to show a degree of autonomy in decision-making. They accept and respect the inevitable levels of review in place for work processes and results. In other words, accountability involves a thorough understanding and deference for following due process, when it is required. Shortcuts and bypassing systems and established practices are not considered an option for someone who is accountable. This respect for due process, however, is tempered by a certain amount of enterprise when it's needed.

For example, during a busy period in a civil engineering firm, there is a tight schedule on an important project. The civil engineers working on this project are reliant on the drafters to supply them with accurate and timely plans to follow in the construction phase. Terry, one of the drafters, is behind on his work and realizes the project director has an important meeting tomorrow with the firm's client.

Terry decides to work late for a few extra hours to get the plans on the desk of the project director before going home that night. He acknowledges that this will assist the project director in creating a favorable impression with the firm's important client at tomorrow's meeting. This is being a team player; recognizing a certain level of personal and team accountability.

Table 7.2 illustrates the KPIs for the element of accountability.

These ten KPIs shown in Table 7.2 are grouped around two competencies. First, there is a *sense of accountability for understanding the importance and value of the work a team member does and the impact that makes to the total team output.* And the second competency is related to being able to *balance the demands* of respecting organizational processes and procedures and displaying initiative when required. These KPIs define what I mean by accountability, the second of the four characteristics involved in the team role.

TABLE 7.2   KPIs for Accountability

Element: Accountability					
Key performance indicators	5	4	3	2	1
1. I readily accept the responsibilities that go with being part of the teams I am a member of.					
2. I don't "point the finger of blame" when things go wrong.					
3. I believe I have the same level of accountability for the team's output as anyone else should hold in the team.					
4. I fully appreciate the impact of the work I do has on the team output.					
5. As part of the process of accountability, I am happy having my work reviewed regularly.					
6. I generally respect the processes and procedures we need to work within the team.					
7. I don't take shortcuts in the team; my work is thorough and I happily accept accountability.					
8. I am able to balance the demands of following organizational processes on the one hand and displaying appropriate initiative on the other hand.					
9. I always feel a sense of responsibility for the team's successes and failures.					
10. I have high standards of what I expect of myself in the teams I belong to.					

Collaboration

Collaboration is the ability to produce successful outcomes by working cooperatively with others. People who have the ability to collaborate understand that this requires some "give and take." We can't always be right, or get our own way; sometimes team members have to accommodate the needs and interests of others. The right frame-of-mind to be genuinely collaborative is to consider the team requirements first, before one's own needs.

An important part of the collaborative process is sharing helpful information in a timely manner with team members. Conversely, it also means soliciting input and assistance from others, when needed. In other words, a collaborator is mindful of constructively contributing to the flow of information. Alternatively, they are prepared to ask relevant questions and seek clarification, drawing upon the expertise or experience of their fellow team members. To do this well, a team member needs to be a good listener and clear communicator. What's more, they are able to integrate the input of others and seek consensus in reaching organizational goals, regardless of their formal status in the team. Team members exhibiting the trait of collaboration take an interest in understanding and respecting their colleagues and the conventions of the team.

For example, the outdoor landscape gardening team for a local government authority had just completed a big gardening job in a large nursing home. Ted, one of the team members, suggested to his boss that they ought to do a quick debrief with the team before moving on to the next project. This team consists of six experienced gardeners. The team leader, Bob, thought it was a good idea and asked Ted to facilitate this debrief. Ted used the *after action review* methodology based on three key questions: *What went well in the project? What didn't go well in the project? What could we do differently next time?* The debrief worked well. Everyone contributed and some great insights and ideas eventuated.

Table 7.3 shows the KPIs associated with the element of collaboration.

The ten KPIs in Table 7.3 are based on three competencies for the element of collaboration. The first competency is a *capacity to work with and through other people* to get the work done. There is a second competency about a *preparedness to share in the decision-making process* through the expression of an opinion or idea. And thirdly, collaboration is not possible without a genuine desire to *listen to the contributions of others* in the team. These KPIs relate to collaboration, the third of four elements associated with the team role.

TABLE 7.3   KPIs for Collaboration

Element: Collaboration					
Key performance indicators	5	4	3	2	1
1. I generally work well with people from diverse backgrounds.					
2. I am willing to accommodate the needs and wishes of other people I work closely with in the interests of achieving a good overall team outcome.					
3. I don't think others that know me well would consider that I have an attitude that "I am always right."					
4. I am very ready to share my thoughts and ideas with my colleagues in a collaborative fashion when the need arises.					
5. If I am not too sure about something, I am willing to ask for help or assistance from my fellow team members.					
6. I think I am generally a good listener.					
7. Wherever possible, I try to seek consensus in the group to achieve important organizational goals.					
8. I enjoy group problem-solving discussions.					
9. I am mostly interested in the views and opinions of others in my team.					
10. I like to make my constructive contribution when the opportunity arises in team meetings.					

Communication

Communication in teams involves effectively interacting and exchanging information with other team members, members of the organization, and external stakeholders, such as suppliers. Specifically, successful communication includes sharing well thought through and timely ideas and opinions based on sound and logical information on the one hand. On the other hand, effective communication is the capacity to engage in meaningful conversation with others when needed. These are the essential verbal communication competencies required. Communication can also cover written expression too, whether this is in the form of reports or emails. It is hard to envisage an employee performing their team role successfully without the ability to communicate in their areas.

Without effective and frequent communication with colleagues, it is going to be challenging to play the team role. In practice, this means speaking up in meetings at the right time, contributing support and assistance when the opportunity arises, and offering constructive advice when asked. Communicating in teams is making sure colleagues are kept well-informed of progress or set-backs affecting the project, and seeking out information that may be useful and important to know. Communication can be carried out through the formal reporting channels, such as set progress meetings, as well as the informal giving and seeking of feedback around the "water cooler." It also, as I mentioned, involves written documentation.

Table 7.4 illustrates the KPIs for communication.

These ten KPIs for the element of communication covered in Table 7.4 contain three competencies. First, some KPIs involve an *awareness of the need to regularly communicate* with team members and members of the wider organizational community. The second competency relates to an ability to *communicate clearly to be understood* by others. And third, a *commitment to listen and respect the views and opinions of others* in the team is also a competency covered in the KPIs. Collectively these KPIs reflect communication, the fourth and final element of the team role.

TABLE 7.4   **KPIs for Communication**

Element: Communication					
Key performance indicators	5	4	3	2	1
1. I make a real effort to constructively communicate with all members of my team on a regular basis.					
2. I am very aware of who our important external stakeholders and suppliers are.					
3. I make an effort to communicate my ideas and opinions to others in a timely, logical, and coherent manner.					
4. My written communication is clear and concise, sharp, and to-the-point.					
5. I generally listen carefully to what others are saying.					
6. I unhesitatingly speak up in team meetings when I have something important to contribute.					
7. I offer support and constructive advice to my boss when I need to.					
8. I keep key people informed of my work and the progress I am making on important assignments.					
9. I am not afraid to ask questions when I need clarification or don't understand.					
10. I am clearly understood by others when I speak.					

A T   T H E   C O A L   F A C E ...

Not on speaking terms in the orchestra

I consult to an orchestra with an outstanding international reputation. To the audience, the orchestra appears to be the epitome of team work. The ensemble is carefully and skillfully conducted by the conductor from the front of the stage. Full-time members of this orchestra are at the top of their game artistically. In fact, some are the very best in their field, whether it is strings, brass, wind, or percussion. But looks and sounds can be deceiving.

Two of the senior members of this particular orchestra had not uttered a single word to each other for over a decade. Not one word! Not in the thousands of rehearsals and concerts they had played in together. Not in the hallway during breaks in rehearsal. Not in the bar celebrating a great concert. Not one word.

These two musicians had had an altercation over artistic standards and this had led to them harboring a misunderstanding about each other. Both musicians blamed the other and elected not to talk to each other. In the event that it was imperative to communicate on an artistic matter, they would pass handwritten notes to each other.

These two musicians sat side-by-side on stage and in rehearsal. That's generally the way it works in orchestras. Your seating position in most sections of an orchestra is set. The closer you are to the front of your section, the more senior you are. The principal musicians sit in the front row. These two musicians shared a music stand too!

I spoke to both musicians separately about this situation and suggested they might consider "breaking the ice" and having a coffee together to seek out their differences. To their credit they did this, and they are now on pretty good speaking terms. But for a long time they were not performing their team role.

In this chapter we have defined the team role, the second of the four non-job roles. I have stated what it is and why the team role is important. Briefly, there are four elements to this competency: Leadership, accountability, collaboration, and communication. Each of these elements – like the other three non-job roles – has certain competencies reflected in the composition of the KPIs. The four tables in this chapter provide 40 KPIs of the team role.

The positive mental attitude and team roles are the two interpersonal non-job roles we have discussed in Chapters 6 and 7 respectively. In the next chapter, we cover the third non-job role and the first of two personal non-job roles; that is, the career development role.

The **Top 10** Key Points ...

1. Given the changing marketplace we work in, cross-functional communication is becoming the dominant mode of communication. These changes in structure and communication require the employee to participate in teams "outside" their functional area; this is now an important part of their work.

2. There are four elements that make up the team role competency. They are: Leadership, accountability, collaboration, and communication.

3. Showing leadership in teams means being able to influence team members in a positive way when the need arises.

4. The KPIs of leadership have three competencies: Influence or persuade others; flexible and open to the ideas of others in the team; and appreciating their team role.

5. Accountability in the context of the team role means accepting the dual responsibility for the work of the team the employee belongs to and their own individual work.

6. The KPIs of accountability have two competencies: A sense of accountability for understanding the importance and value of their work and the impact that makes to the total team output, and balancing the demands of respecting organizational processes and procedures and displaying initiative when required.

7. Collaboration is the ability to produce successful outcomes by working cooperatively with others.

8. The KPIs of collaboration have three competencies: A capacity to work with and through other people to get the work done; a preparedness to share in the decision-making process; and a genuine desire to listen to the contributions of others in the team.

9. Communication in teams involves effectively interacting and exchanging information with other team members, members of the organization, and external stakeholders, such as suppliers.

The KPIs of communication have three competencies: An awareness of the need to regularly communicate with team members and members of the wider organizational community; an ability to communicate clearly to be understood by others; and a commitment to listen and respect the views and opinions of others in the team.

8

chapter

The Career Development Role

The wise 21st-century employee makes independent career management decisions for guiding the purpose and direction of their work-life.

Now that senior management has shown its faith in her abilities by promoting her to lead the front-of-house team at the theatre, Jocelyn is determined to be the best line manager she can be. She knows her mentor from the HR department, Sue, must have had a lot to do with her promotion. She recruited her to the theatre complex three years ago and seems to have taken a personal interest in her success since then.

She is always friendly, never failing to take a few minutes to chat about the goings-on in the complex, plans for forthcoming events, personnel movements between the departments, and so on. Several times she requested that Jocelyn be put on project teams looking into various aspects of client service and productivity. This gives Jocelyn a broad understanding of the workings of the theatre complex and exposes her to people from every department at all levels. She also arranged for her to undertake a few project assignments in different areas of the theatre, and nominated her to be on a high-profile enterprise bargaining working group.

Jocelyn made the most of these opportunities, learning everything she could and contributing as she felt able to. She tried to "dress the part" when she was on these special committees and teams; in fact, she took her cues from the way Sue dressed. She was friendly and cheerful with everyone and made a conscious effort to keep up her contacts with people after the project teams disbanded.

In this way, Jocelyn had gradually become known throughout the theatre complex as a dedicated, hardworking, and cheerful employee who added value wherever she went. Her manager appreciated Jocelyn's efforts too. Jocelyn always presented information in writing, with plenty of facts and statistics, as she sensed her manager preferred information in writing with no holding back on the details. Jocelyn also made an effort to suggest good ideas and tried hard to motivate and energize the rest of the team.

When the time came for Jocelyn's manager to move on from supervising the front-of-house, there were ringing endorsements all round of Sue's recommendation that Jocelyn take on the role.[1]

Continually growing and developing as an employee and a person is imperative, not only for the individual, but also for the organization that employs them. Improving one's skills-set preserves and amplifies the currency of the employee's capabilities and so, their employability. Simultaneously, a more skilled and capable workforce – committed to continuously learning – is an asset to any organization. The career development role – like the other three roles – is essential to the performance of the individual and organization. Gone are the days when you could get a qualification and close the book, so to speak, and stop learning. "Leaving your brains in a paper bag" at the doorway of the undergraduate academic program or apprenticeship is not an option anymore. A critically important factor in the success of the 20th-century employee was very much about obtaining some form of certification or qualification; that was the "meal ticket." The successful 21st-century employee still needs this foundational accreditation, but – in addition – is continuously learning and growing and able to flexibly deploy their skills-set in a variety of contexts and situations. Constant growth, adaptability, and development replace the qualification as the winning career factor now.

Despite the importance of ongoing career development today, it astonishes me how many people decide to stop improving themselves and rest on their current skills-set. I hear people frequently saying things like: "I'm too old to learn." Or others say something along the lines of: "I'm happy to do this task; I'm not really interested in learning something new." Out of fear of failure from learning something new or wanting to believe that learning is a one-off event, rather than an ongoing process, many employees stop learning and developing.

To compound this "I don't want to learn anymore" attitude, the employer can no longer offer the employee job security. Add to this, the corporate career path is not as commonplace as it once was. Using a *ladder* as a metaphor, the corporate ladder is much shorter than it once was, and it's leaning against a wobbly wall. In other words, there are fewer promotional opportunities and less certainty about the availability of those prospects today. The apparent and predictable work promotion model – or career ladder – stressing job security and an organizationally-based career path, is a vestige of the last century. A broader, less predictable pathway reinforces the need for continuous learning and individualized career development in the 21st century.

The logical employee response to this present landscape of job insecurity and reduced internal promotional opportunities is to take charge of their own career. The modern employee defines work success on their own terms. Although there are undoubtedly less rungs to climb on the corporate ladder, there is nonetheless a wider array of career options and different pathway possibilities than ever before. And progressing up the ranks of an organization – once the universal measure of career success – is now only one of a multitude of ways society-at-large defines career success.

Changes in economic, social, and technological advances are putting considerable pressure on the organization to be malleable and responsive. A more maneuverable organizational structure has a greater capacity to meet competitive global market transformations. Most contemporary enterprises have reacted to these unrelenting and pervasive forces by trimming costs and improving efficiencies. Enterprises everywhere across all industries are downsizing, restructuring, and de-layering their work-force. There is very little "fat" in organizational systems nowadays.

Everyone I come across complains they are short-staffed and have too much to do and too little time to do it. Apart from the new management mantra of "doing more with less," priorities are not as clear-cut and are in a continual state of re-evaluation. The employee is justifiably feeling the pinch too. Employment insecurity and career discontinuity replaces employment security and career continuity across all industries, at all levels, in all geographic locations.

Consequently, there is a transformation taking place in the employment relationship. The emerging psychological contract is starting to resemble the eight values of the new employment relationship model I illustrated and discussed in Chapter 4. Although, as I have said, I think the dominant psychological contract of most enterprises is still in a transitional phase between the old and new models. But generally speaking, the evolution is one of going from a long-term working relationship – based on a value of loyalty – to one of a short-term transactional relationship, character-ized by the idea of "you scratch my back and I'll scratch yours." With a less predictable marketplace and an evolving employment relationship, it is understandable that the employee wants to take a hands-on approach to their own career development. Leaving the responsibility of their career development in the hands of their current employer is risky and impractical.

Protean career

This idea of the employee proactively looking after their career, instead of waiting for the organization to do so, was originally labeled the "pro-tean career" by Douglas Hall, a distinguished professor in management.[2] The protean career is a career where the individual employee takes most of the responsibility for their vocational choices and opportunities. The values supporting the protean career are diametrically opposite to the traditional ladder-climbing career path.

The beliefs of the organizational-sponsored career path are loyalty and compliance; loyalty to the employer and compliance to the systems, practices, and culture adopted and espoused by the business. At the other end of the spectrum, the values underpinning the protean career are predominantly independence and initiative. By independence I mean the acknowledgement by the employee that they are the custodian of making career decisions and choices. And by initiative, I mean that the employee is proactive in making those decisions and choices about their career. Personal choice and individual responsibility are the defining qualities of the protean career.

This doesn't completely let the organization "off the hook" when it comes to the career development of their employees. The organization still has an important – albeit different – role to play in the growth and development of the employee's career. This organizationally-sponsored HRD responsibility is more than skilling-up and grooming employees to take on internal job opportunities. HRD now must venture beyond the provision of learning and development tools to prepare the employee for the technical requirements of their current, and even future, anticipated organizational jobs. But even with a more comprehensive organizationally-driven career development program, a large chunk of the burden has shifted from the organization to the individual.

AT THE COAL FACE ...

Protean career

Chin and Rasdi, two notable academics, define the protean career in this passage from their paper, "Protean Career Development: Exploring the Individuals, Organizational and Job-related Factors," this way:

"The word 'protean' is derived after 'Proteus', the Greek sea-god who could change and transform in many shapes or substances at will (Hall, 1976). The protean individuals value individual freedom and self-growth; and define career success in term of psychological factors, such as the degree of job satisfaction, self-actualization, personal accomplishment and sense of self-fulfilment (Hall & Chandler, 2005). In a similar vein, Briscoe and Hall (2006) explained that a protean career emphasizes two important dimensions, which are value driven and self-directedness. Value driven attitude refers to 'a person's internal values that provide the guidance and measurement of success for individual career' (Briscoe & Hall, 2006, p. 8). The latter refers to 'one who is adaptive in terms of performance and learning demands' (Briscoe & Hall, 2006, p. 8). The notion of protean career is to emphasize that individuals take charge to manage their career. In addition, the protean career individual is continuously learning and anticipates work challenges in pursuing career paths (Briscoe & Hall, 2006)."[3]

The performance significance of the career development role can be understood from an historical perspective. How did the shift from the traditional career path to the protean career take place? In the 1950s and 1960s, the emphasis on hierarchical and rigid organizing structures was the foundation for the vertical career path. Indeed, the organizational hierarchy was the ladder to climb to achieve career success. Stability of structure and the lucidity of the career ladder formed the framework for career progression. Against this backdrop the employee didn't need to take their career into their own hands; it was done for them by the organization. A career path in those days was illustrated in the organizational chart.

Growth and development for an ambitious employee centered on mastering a specific set of job-skills. Basically this learning was about acquiring the skills to step into their boss's job. Career development was predominantly an employee replacing their manager when they moved up the hierarchy, or out of the organization. Succession planning was a straightforward exercise; that is, to prepare the employee to eventually replace their boss. The job description reinforced this message, and still does, to a certain extent.

In the 1970s, the Baby Boomer generation was just starting out in their careers. This post-war cohort has a different set of values from their mothers and fathers. Baby Boomers wanted – and still do – freedom, personal choice, and self-expression. These values are somewhat reflected in their workplace career choice. For instance, this generation showed an active interest in self-development and started to question the relevance of the conventional career ladder. Questions such as, *Do I want to do this line-of-work for the rest of my life? Am I personally suited to this work? Is the career ladder the only option available to me?* were being asked for the first time by the post-war generation. HRD opportunities were still largely dictated by the resources of the employer. But the Baby Boomer employee started to critically evaluate these organizationally-led programs for their more adventurous career aspirations.

Some companies were quick to respond to this new focus on freedom, personal choice, and self-expression and most are doing so today. To remain relevant to the changes in career aspirations, HRD practices started to align individual career development and organizational career management. The aim being two-fold. First, this alliance reflected the rise of the protean career and its emphasis on individual learning and development. And second, this matching of individual and organizational needs was about building the business's human resource capabilities for a competitive advantage in the marketplace. The aim of moving from organizational to individual development was to achieve an optimal match and "fit" between individual and organization. This changing emphasis of HRD accommodated the rise of the protean career and the competitive needs of the business.

This HRD momentum accelerated in the 1990s and 2000s with the gargantuan movement to outsourcing human capital. The outsourcing of human resources on a needs basis – along with other influences – hastened the changing psychological contract between employer and employee. In particular, the outsourcing movement was the catalyst for the development of the protean career. Proactive career self-management became the norm in career development. Today, most employees investigate and acquire the necessary skills and personal development they need for their career plans.

The wise 21st-century employee makes independent career management decisions for guiding the purpose and direction of their work-life. Likewise, organizational leaders understand and accommodate the employee's self-driven quest for employability; they mostly accept their new management responsibility in career development. The shared value in the new contract between employee and manager is commitment, one of the eight values of the new employment relationship (see Chapter 4). What the value of commitment means is that the organization commits to assisting the employee to achieve their personal objectives, including career development. And in exchange, the value of commitment means the employee commits to assisting the organization to achieve its objectives. With the shared value of commitment, both entities in the employment relationship have a stake in career development.

So, even though career management and development has fundamentally shifted from employer to employee, the organization still has a significant, but different, role to play. To illustrate the importance of the organizational role in career development, research indicates that employee career success is enhanced when organizations take this new role seriously. Specifically, the research showed that organizations with formal policies and practice in place for managing careers were more helpful for employees than those without any policies, or merely informal policies.[4] Employees in this study considered that they had better careers in organizations that offered wide-ranging career information and advice. Significantly, organizations that provided comprehensive career information were not necessarily considered better businesses than enterprises that didn't provide such information.

This research suggests employee career success is still dependent to some extent on the company that offers career development opportunities and support. Relevant HRD that the average employee is not able to access and pay for is going to be attractive to the employee. A comprehensive career development program provides the employee with information, motivation, and support; it is not just about salary increases and ladder-climbing. This research reminds us that even though the employee is now taking control of their career, this is not a signal for the organization to completely abandon their career development obligations. As tempting as it may

A comprehensive career development program provides the employee with information, motivation, and support; it is not just about salary increases and ladder-climbing.

AT THE COAL FACE ...

Career development as a retention strategy

GHD is an infrastructure and project consultancy firm. Their approach to formal training is based on a "business school" model that encompasses technical training, management and leadership, and personal development. This format allows economies-of-scale and consistency across business units. Training can be for skills required for specific projects or for career development.

Here is how the General Manager and Director, Australia and New Zealand, describes the program: "It's a virtual business school so you know it doesn't have a very big campus somewhere but it has a whole heap of programs some of which we have tailored and developed ourselves, others which we have outsourced. All with the objective of developing our people through their career to 1) meet our future needs but also so they meet their own aspirations. If you go back to what I said originally, these people are in enormous demand. If they don't get the sense they are developing to their full potential at GHD they'll leave. It is more than just getting the skills we need in the future; it's an integral part of keeping them with us."[5]

appear, disbanding career development opportunities and diverting these resources into other areas of the business will be counterproductive.

Attracting and retaining talent shows up consistently in surveys as one of the most important HR challenges that businesses are facing. Ironically, organizations that encourage and support the protean career concept improve their capacity to attract and retain employees. By effectively helping employees explore a wide range of career options, the sponsoring employer is stimulating employees' motivation and assisting with their development. An extensive career development program can paradoxically lead to the employee staying with their current employer longer than may otherwise be the case. A well thought through, organizationally-sponsored HRD program that is based on the career needs of the individual can serve as an employee retention (and attraction) strategy, as irrational as this may sound. I have more to say about this in my book, *Attracting and Retaining Talent: Becoming an Employer of Choice.*[6]

Rewards and recognition have a role to play in career development too. You'll recall that in the last chapter I spoke of rewards and remuneration in the context of teams. The saying that "what gets rewarded gets done," is pretty much true. If we reward teamwork we consequently get more teamwork, and if we reward individualism we get more individualistic behavior.

In the career context, some organizations are rewarding employees for career accomplishments, either directly through pay increases, or indirectly by providing further career development opportunities. These rewards are often linked with training and educational achievements. For instance, skill-based pay is connected to the career development role. These pay programs provide employees with bonuses or increases in their base salary when they acquire new competencies or attain further qualifications. The companies who use rewards such as skill-based pay, recognize that the application of these newly acquired competencies positively impact organizational performance, either directly or indirectly.

Skills and knowledge gained and used by employees builds organizational capacity. In other words, the ongoing growth and development of the employee is not only doing their career and themselves a favor, but is doing their current employer a favor too. An employee taking charge of their own career and building personal capacity is in the interests of more than just the employee.

In the workplace, career development can take many forms. For example, there is multi-skilling, up-skilling, rotating jobs, and so on. Supporting the protean career, and encouraging and assisting the employee to develop, benefits the organization. This is essentially the rationale for including the career development role in the non-job roles framework. My criticism of the job description in this context is that it is so job-centric that it is not geared toward career development *per se*.

There are two elements that make up the career development competency:

- Technical development.
- Personal development.

Both are important for career success.

Briefly, the first element – and the most apparent – is technical development; that is, the building of a job-related skills-set. This set-of-skills is necessary to accomplish an employee's current or future job role; they represent the practical requirements of the job. The second element of this role is personal development. I defined the personal development or the person-centered dimension of learning and development in Chapter 5. Personal development is building competencies that enable a person to be more effective and efficient as a person and so, indirectly, a better employee too. Although a brief introduction, I'll define these two elements of the career development role in more detail below.

Technical development

By undergoing some form of *technical development*, an employee is endeavoring to enhance their capacity to do their present and future jobs better. The technical element of career enhancement could include either learning an entirely new skills-set or boosting a current competency.

Technical development can cover a wide spectrum of activity from enrolling in a formal training program or course-of-study through to an informal and spontaneous coaching session on-the-job. Developing skills and knowledge can be practical or theoretical in its orientation, or a combination of both. It may involve, for instance, studying a predetermined curriculum delivered online or in a classroom or learning hands-on tasks on-the-job, or a blend of the two. The learning environment can be a classroom or conference setting off-site or in the workplace "at the coal face." There are numerous ways and means of attaining technical competence.

Developing technically in a protean career means planning and making decisions about education, training, and career choices by the employee. It is ultimately the individual's responsibility to seek out and take up opportunities to improve or learn new technical competencies within and outside the business they are currently working in. Career learning and development is an ongoing, never-ending process of research, discovery, application, and review. Technical development is more than enrolling in and completing formal course work. Career development does require an employee to commit to life-long learning.

To illustrate, Pam works in administration at head office of a large government department. She enjoys her job and realizes that she must continually upgrade her skills and knowledge, particularly with the ever increasing number of software programs she is expected to use at work. Pam asks her manager if she could attend a one-day workshop on *Excel*. She had sourced this information online and is keen to learn how to use some of the advanced features of the software. Pam's skills in Excel are adequate; but she wanted to improve her knowledge, foreseeing opportunities to use this software more extensively in her current administrative role. Her boss understands the benefits too and she attends the program, one of many throughout her career.

In Table 8.1, I have listed ten KPIs for the element of technical development.

The KPIs in Table 8.1 are based on two competencies relevant to technical development. First, some of the ten statements are related to an *attitude of proactively seeking out opportunities* to grow and develop work-related

TABLE 8.1   KPIs for Technical development

Element: Technical development					
Key performance indicators	**5**	**4**	**3**	**2**	**1**
1. I am always seeking out opportunities to improve my job-related skills.					
2. I enthusiastically attend skill-based training programs to enhance the job I do.					
3. I would describe myself as very coachable when shown how to do something new at work.					
4. I am always keen to take up opportunities to upgrade my job skills-set.					
5. I am always looking for better ways to do my job more efficiently and effectively.					
6. I enjoy learning new skills related to my job.					
7. Continuously improving and upgrading my ability to do my job is a priority for me.					
8. Over the past 12 months, I have undertaken some form of learning or training related to my job.					
9. I enjoy learning new, and improving existing, job skills that assist me in my career.					
10. I have discussed my opportunities for growth in my job and ways of enhancing my skills in those areas with my boss.					

skills. And second, the other statements tell of a *willingness to undertake learning opportunities* – whenever they present themselves – to improve a career skills-set. These KPIs affect technical development, the first of two elements linked to the career development role.

Let's now look at the second element of the career development role: Personal development.

Personal development

What is the difference between technical development and *personal development*? While technical development is about directly improving competencies connected to a specific job, personal development is about developing the person. By developing oneself, the person is – in a roundabout way – developing their capabilities at work.

For instance, learning project management skills can help an engineer be a better engineer. Or learning time management skills can assist a manager to prioritize their work. Or learning some skills in emotional intelligence can improve a salesperson's ability to deal with people. Personal development is the less popular of the two elements of career development, but is integral to work performance, all the same.

Developing oneself helps in carrying out employment duties. Similar to developing technical competence, employees committed to improving themselves actively seek out suitable opportunities to expand their knowledge, skills, and experience. In terms of the protean career, the employee commits to their own personal development, understanding that it is nobody else's responsibility but their own.

But it is possible that an employee can have a great technical skills-set and ignore the relevance of personal development for career progression; many do this to their detriment. By neglecting the personal development dimension, the employee is not totally fulfilling their career development role, not to mention their potential. Both elements are important.

Consider Fred. He lacked confidence when he was around other people, particularly those he didn't know, or know well. This was a problem for him. Fred is in a sales role for his company. There was no doubting his technical knowledge; it was "cutting edge." Fred knows every aspect of the "white goods" he sells in the retail outlet. This is because he was originally a refrigeration mechanic; he decided to change occupations and become a salesperson owing to a crook back.

Fred joined an organization called *Toastmasters* and gradually learnt the skills of speaking in public. After several years – and lots of impromptu and prepared speeches – he developed into an outstanding public speaker. But more notably in terms of his sales role, Fred's confidence improved remarkably. This in turn helped him circuitously improve his ability to sell. Fred now sells a lot more refrigerators than he once did.

He worked hard on his personal development – specifically his ability to speak in public – and it helped Fred ultimately improve his ability to do the job he was employed to do.

In Table 8.2 are the ten KPIs for the element of personal development.

The KPIs in Table 8.2 are based on two competencies. They are similar to the competencies for technical development. Many of the statements are related to an *attitude of wanting to continually grow and develop* as a person. The other statements are related to *actively seeking out opportunities to grow and develop* personally. Collectively, these KPIs are linked

TABLE 8.2   KPIs for Personal development

Element: Personal development					
Key performance indicators	5	4	3	2	1
1. I am always striving for ways and means to develop as a person.					
2. I continuously seek out opportunities to improve myself as a person.					
3. I enjoy learning things that assist me to grow and develop as a person.					
4. As far as I am concerned, it is my responsibility to constantly grow as a person.					
5. I am always on the lookout for ways to improve who I am as a person and how I interact with my surroundings.					
6. I always try to put into practice personal development skills I have learnt.					
7. I hold the view that I will never lose the desire to stop growing as a person.					
8. Over the past 12 months, I have undertaken some form of personal development.					
9. Growing and developing as a person is an important value of mine.					
10. I have discussed my opportunities for personal growth with my boss, and ways to improve in these areas.					

to personal development, the second of the two elements of the career development role.

In this chapter, I have explained what the career development role consists of. The career development role is the third of the four non-job roles in the framework. I have defined what it involves and why it's becoming increasingly important for both the individual and the organization. Briefly, the two elements of the career development role are technical development and personal development. Both of these elements require similar competencies: A willingness to develop and a preparedness to find opportunities to grow technical and personal capabilities. The two tables in this chapter combine to form 20 KPIs for the career development role.

The career development role is the first of the two personal non-job roles. In the next chapter we cover the fourth non-job role and the second of two personal non-job roles; that is, the innovation and continuous improvement role.

The **Top 10** Key Points ...

1. Continually growing and developing, as an employee and personally, is imperative – not only for the individual, but also for the organization that employs them.

2. Gone are the days when you could get a qualification and close the book – so to speak – and stop learning.

3. This idea of the employee proactively looking after their career instead of waiting for the organization to do so was originally labeled the "protean career" by Douglas Hall.

4. The outsourcing movement was the catalyst for the development of the protean career. Proactive career self-management became the norm in career development.

5. Even though career management and development has fundamentally shifted from employer to employee, the organization still has a significant, but different, role to play.

6. Organizations that encourage and support the protean career concept improve their capacity to attract and retain employees.

7 The two elements that make up the career development competency are technical development and personal development.

8 By undergoing some form of technical development, an employee is endeavoring to enhance their capacity to do their present and future jobs better.

9 While technical development is about directly improving competencies connected to a specific job, personal development is about developing the person.

10 Both of the two elements of the career development role require similar competencies: A willingness to develop and a preparedness to find opportunities to grow technical and personal capabilities.

9

The Innovation and Continuous Improvement Role

The employee is brainwashed into accepting and carrying out systems and processes to the letter, meeting their task-related KPIs, and not displaying too much original thought or enterprise.

"Spotify" is an example of a company that spotted a gap in the market and exploited it through creative and innovative thinking. The subscription music service allows paying users to stream unlimited music on their computers and phones. Launched at a time when piracy was at a high level, and people were reluctant to pay a large amount to download music, the service addressed a clear new market, and offered individuals an affordable and revolutionary way to enjoy high quantities of music, without having to resort to illegal downloads.

To increase idea generation, the Pitney Bowes Credit Corporation wanted to improve communication between their employees. The company decided to completely redesign the interior office space to resemble a calm, small village. The idea was to break down communication barriers. The redesigned office had its own village square and café, which was designed to encourage trust and a feeling of community among employees. The relaxed workplace saw the company go from strength to strength, launching successful new products because of increased collaboration and communication levels.

All professional sport is now business because of the vast amounts of sponsorship money involved. In cycling, "Team Sky" used innovation to great success in 2012 to pull off one of the greatest British sporting feats of all time in winning the Tour de France. Dave Brailsford, Performance Director for British Cycling, put the success down to a strategy of incremental improvements. The team took the innovative approach of making tiny improvements in all areas, going to unprecedented extremes, like ordering a custom-made, skin-tight, leader's yellow jersey for Bradley Wiggins to wear in time trials. The philosophy was that these slight changes would gradually add up, ultimately proving to be the difference between success and failure.[1]

In a world of rapid and relentless change, enterprises and individuals can't endure unless they constantly improve themselves. In the previous chapter, we looked at growth and development of the employee and their career. In this chapter, we look at growth and development of the organization. By growth and development, I am referring to new and better systems, processes, and practices of the business. The very best companies are in a continual state of improvement; they are always looking for ways and means of getting better and being more responsive to the needs of their customers.

As we are constantly reminded by the glut of management books, articles, and blogs, a company's ideas for innovation and continuous improvement should come from tapping its employees. So an increasingly important role of the manager is to harvest these ideas and suggestions. But we both know this is not as straightforward as it sounds. I haven't come across too many companies where the mass of employees are eagerly blurting out their thoughts and ideas for business improvement. More typically, employees complain about "this, that, and the other"; when challenged to come up with a better approach or solution, they go silent. I think many employees buy into the old employment contract that business improvement is the boss's responsibility.

To contribute to business improvement, employees need to think a certain way; for starters, they are never entirely satisfied with the *status quo*, always on the lookout for enhancement. The innovation and continuous improvement role puts the spotlight squarely on the value and importance of this attitude; having the right attitude is the beginning of change. Yet the standard job description doesn't really elaborate on the employee's responsibility for organization development. And if the innovation and continuous improvement role does get mentioned in the job description, it is usually only superficially covered, with no precise benchmarks for success. So it is hardly surprising that there's not a free flow of business improvement ideas and suggestions generated from most employees in most businesses.

Organization development discussions are not a high priority in most companies; managers and employees are usually too busy making the current system work to bother with how it might be modified! Take the formal performance review, for example. In these dreaded appraisal meetings – generally conducted once or twice a year – ideas for business improvement are avoided, or there is no time left at the end of the meeting to discuss them. Again, how often is business improvement a topic on the agenda of the typical weekly work-in-progress meeting? Rarely, if at all, I would respond, with some confidence. Sometimes a bright idea floats to the surface at the water cooler, but it's not often followed up.

So employees are understandably left with a clear impression that workplace innovation and continuous improvement is a secondary consideration, at best, and not really part of their job. Of greater significance – in the minds of the employee and their manager – is meeting the KPIs in their job description. This is universally considered the first – and often only – ingredient in employment success.

What's more, on the rare occasion a discussion about improving the working environment takes place at a team meeting, the wrong questions are asked by the manager. Thoughtful and open-ended questions such as: *How can we complete our tasks faster/with fewer errors/with reduced cost/with higher quality/with more customer responsiveness?*

are rarely asked, let alone satisfactorily answered. Instead, superficial and generalized questions are posed, such as: *Does anyone have any suggestions for improvement?* Muted silence inevitably follows and the manager gives up on the idea of discussing organization development issues at team meetings from that point on. Another powerful inhibitor of innovation and improvement is the concentration on compliance and conformity in the workplace. The employee is brainwashed into accepting and carrying out systems and processes to the letter, meeting their task-related KPIs, and not displaying too much original thought or enterprise. This conditioning makes the employee complacent. Understandably, the employee has no interest, energy, or time to genuinely explore better, faster, or easier ways of producing services or products. But simultaneously, the rhetoric is different; the employee is told repeatedly that innovation and improvement is vital in a fast-changing and competitive world. The employee receives mixed messages.

Workplace improvement paradox

I call this mixed messaging the *workplace improvement paradox*. The paradox works like this: The manager wants the employee to play an active role in making improvements to the business. Likewise, the employee starts out keen to offer their suggestions for organizational efficiency and effectiveness. The manager proceeds to invite constructive suggestions at a team meeting. Someone offers a suggestion in response, and the manager replies saying that it has been tried and doesn't work. No other suggestions come up; the other employees don't want to incur the same response. Nothing happens. So the manager doesn't bother asking again, thinking that the team members are not interested in organization development. As the subject is not raised again by the manager, the employee thinks their manager is not really interested in their suggestions; after all, if the manager was concerned, they would ask more often. And the workplace improvement paradox begins and the cycle of inactivity is reinforced.

Not all companies suffer from the workplace improvement paradox. Some businesses strike a healthy balance between the need to be innovative and striving to regularly improve, and respecting and following established systems and practices. Take *Apple* as a well-known example. Apple is widely considered to be a company highly committed to innovation. Employees take their innovation and continuous improvement role seriously; they are encouraged and expected to contribute ideas. It is therefore hardly surprising that Apple is, more often than not, first to market with technical and design innovations. The company, for example, was the first to commercialize touch screen technology. Innovation is a core value for Apple employees, and speed to market is a hallmark of the corporation. Other businesses have tried – and many have failed – to imitate this commitment to innovation and continuous improvement. But why? Why has Apple succeeded and others failed?

Most organizations are still locked into the stability and predictability mindset of the last century. And this state-of-mind restrains critical thinking and creativity. In a stable and predictable work environment, the manager beds down lots of processes and procedures; they expect employees to follow these practices, without question. The rationalization for adhering to these systems is that they are the best way to accomplish work-related tasks. Under these constraints, it is impossible to expect employees to think creatively. One of these straightjackets is the job description.

This mindset, reinforced through generations of employees, confuses the contemporary employee about their organizational role. The employee is supposed to follow standard operating procedures, but at the same time, the employee is supposed to be enterprising; always striving to improve existing processes. For the pragmatic employee, the upshot of this dilemma is to default to the *status quo*; that is, follow standard operating practices. By taking this path, employees are following what they perceive as the safest route. But it favors compliance over enterprise.

But the reality is this: Things are moving so fast in the modern marketplace that the business that prospers is the one that is adaptable, flexible, and nimble. The 21st-century business wants and needs their employees to be enterprising in the way they think about, and carry out, their work. So why do most managers still want the employee to follow standardized processes? I think it's about control.

Managers measure and monitor an employee's performance against a predictable set of criteria. We live in a world obsessed with measurable standards and we consequently like to evaluate the employee against these norms. There is an understandable attraction for the traditionally-minded manager to simplify and regulate the work of the employee through a set of KPIs. But beyond the work tasks embedded in the job description, there are usually no KPIs around business improvement. Yet the rate of acceleration and change in the marketplace requires a transformational approach to work. The employee has to embrace change and improvement. This means the manager must let go of their addiction to compliance and push for what is referred to as *constructive disobedience*.[2]

Constructive disobedience

Constructive disobedience is a way of thinking and acting. It ought to be encouraged – or at the very least, not discouraged – by organizational leaders. The manager provides the necessary support for the employee to perform their innovation and continuous improvement role. More specifically, the manager should highlight where improvement is needed most; they ought to then create time and space for the employee to come up with better ways of doing things. The manager must ask carefully targeted questions and genuinely welcome any, and all, responses. Furthermore, one of the manager's primary functions is to encourage employees to critically evaluate everything in the business. Business improvement must be a priority and regular agenda item for meetings. Leading by example is crucial; it is not to be underestimated. Employees need to see their leaders being constructively disobedient too. In brief, the manager has to champion divergent thinking, fresh ideas, and "off the wall" suggestions.

All decisions at work can be classified three ways. Some decisions are clear-cut. In these situations, the appropriate response is to follow a standard operating procedure without question. For example, most decisions within the realm of safety belong in this category. At the other end of the decision-making spectrum, some decisions require a display of initiative; these situations warrant an original response to a unique workplace problem. For example, a customer comes up to the reception-ist in a five-star hotel and asks for a copy of the recipe of a meal he has just consumed in the hotel's main restaurant. The answer to what to do is unlikely to be in a procedures manual under the counter! What should the receptionist do? What would you do? These two types of decisions represent the extremes on the decision-making spectrum.

The third type of decision is more challenging. In these situations, the employee is placed in a predicament; they are faced with these questions: *Do I follow set procedures or do I show some initiative? Which is the best course-of-action?* This category is where decision-making can go one of two ways; the solution can either be to follow protocol or to abandon protocol. The right decision is a judgment call.

For example, consider Bethany, an employee in charge of purchasing product in a large corporation with stringent purchasing rules and regula-tions. One of those policies is to order products at a specified time each month. But Bethany has heard from one of her reliable contacts that the company she works for has won a lucrative contract with a large customer. This customer requires urgent delivery of the product. Bethany elects to order outside the normal ordering cycle in response to the immediate need of the customer. This enterprising behavior exhibited by Bethany violates a major company policy. It is, however, in the interests of the customer and ultimately, the company.

People often fail to show initiative in a quandary such as this; in situations that are neither clear-cut nor completely open to enterprising behavior. In the above case, Bethany was put in a position where she could have justifiably played it safe by following the procedures manual. It is in these situations, where things are not necessarily "black and white" that managers find it challenging to promote appropriate initiative in employees. These "gray" or ambiguous areas or situations ought to be reviewed immediately after they arise. They can be discussed in team meetings or be the topic of conversation one-on-one when the opportunity presents itself. By raising these circumstances where decisions are not straightforward, agreement can be reached and understanding developed between the employee and their manager. Similar future situations can then be approached with more confidence and certainty.

To sum up this discussion, there isn't an industry anywhere on the planet that wouldn't benefit from change and development. Performing an innovation and continuous improvement role is imperative for all organizational members. Finding different and superior ways of approaching issues specific to a workplace is everyone's business.

Difference between innovation and continuous improvement

Before we move on to identify and discuss the core elements of this non-job role, I would like to make clear the distinction between innovation and continuous improvement. *Continuous improvement*, as the phrase implies, is progressively making improvements in the way things are being done. In other words, continuous improvement in the workplace is about refining and improving the way we go about the work that needs doing; it is about improving something, not replacing it. Key questions for continuous improvement include: *How can this be done quicker/with greater accuracy/in a more timely fashion/with more "buy-in"/in a more cost-effective way?* Briefly, continuous improvement is concerned with building on what is already in place.

Innovation is a different concept; it is about coming up with an entirely new way of doing something. To innovate, you use a different thought process. While continuous improvement is focused on building upon what is already in place, innovation is concerned with the question: *Is there a completely new and more efficient and effective way of resolving this issue or completing this task?* Putting it another way, innovation is transforming something, whereas continuous improvement is conserving and improving upon what we already have.

AT THE COAL FACE ...

Flush with cash: Saving fuel costs

British Airways (BA) is saving US$896,000 a year in fuel costs by de-scaling the toilet pipes on its planes and making them lighter. This brainwave is one of the more unusual innovations from BA employees to help reduce emissions and cut fuel costs. BA said the costs in savings were worth more than US$30 million – the flight cost of 550 flights from London to New York.

Other ideas out of the 200 submitted, included replacing glass with plastic for wine bottles, reducing the volume of water tanks, washing engines more regularly, lighter catering trolleys and cargo containers, and introducing lighter cutlery for business class passengers. The airline also employed more conventional methods, such as reducing the use of auxiliary power units, single engine taxiing and performance improvement packages on more than 40 Boeing 777 aircraft.

Jonathon Counseli, Head of Environment at British Airways, said: "This really has been a team effort. It goes to show that small changes here and there can add up to significant savings. Not only does this help us to reduce our environmental impact, it also saves us money."[3]

It can seem a daunting task to know where to begin; where do we start looking for new or better ways of doing organizational work? Instead of concentrating attention on the most obscure places, the best place to begin the journey of organization development is actually in the most obvious places; the time-consuming routine tasks that people do daily. The usual, everyday, mundane tasks that consume large chunks of employees' time are the area to focus on. Why? Small, incremental changes on tasks that absorb large slabs of labor time can have significant dividends in the long term.

Here are some areas open for innovation and continuous improvement. Starting with *"How can we..."*:

- *improve* quality?
- *reduce* time?
- *reduce* costs?
- *increase* output?
- *increase* safety?
- *meet* deadlines?
- *enhance* interpersonal cooperation?
- *streamline* systems and processes?

This is not a comprehensive list. But these pointers do focus the mind on areas of business that are essential and possibly open for change or improvement.

After selecting an area, more probing questions can be asked. For example, consider interpersonal cooperation; an area that is often neglected in organization development:

- How can we improve interpersonal cooperation between our team and other teams in the company?
- What are the barriers that get in the way of cooperation between teams?
- What are some of the opportunities open to us to improve interpersonal cooperation?
- What would be the first step?

These sort of thought-provoking questions are a good place to begin.

Let's now turn to the elements of the role. There are two essential elements that are important in exercising the innovation and continuous improvement role. These elements are:

- Problem-solving and critical thinking.
- Customer responsiveness.

Briefly, to be able to solve problems and think critically assists the employee in considering the requirements for facing work-related challenges, and decisively evaluating the current circumstances. The second element, customer responsiveness, is concerned with being receptive to the needs of internal and external customers. The employee that is competent in carrying out this element is able to consider their products and services consistently from the perspective of the customer, and able to adjust their response accordingly. Further, customer responsiveness opens up the possibility of improving the customer experience. Similar to the other three non-job roles covered in the previous chapters, I will define these two elements in more detail below to get a better overall understanding of the role.

Problem-solving and critical thinking

Problem-solving and critical thinking is having the capacity not only to find solutions to challenging problems in the workplace, but to be able to constructively think through their application. People who can't or won't problem-solve and think critically usually seek out others for the answers in the first instance; usually their boss. Furthermore, employees without this capacity usually want prescriptive answers to resolving dilemmas in the workplace, whether they warrant them or not.

Conversely, employees who are adept at problem-solving are prepared to consider an array of possible solutions; they enjoy the challenge; they have the capacity to reflect critically on what and how solutions may or may not work. These traits are evident when the employee frequently seeks to identify, define, critically analyze, and resolve work problems through investigation and testing of alternative ideas and approaches. This non-job role – more than the other three – involves thinking beyond traditional parameters; it involves using innovative and creative ideas and actions to improve work processes, particularly regarding the customer-interface. The appropriate mindset for performing the innovation and improvement role is one of seldom settling for a service or process that is "good enough." Employees with this attitude strive to add value and take measured risks in their work.

In one of my previous books, *The End of the Performance Review: A New Approach to Appraising Employee Performance*,[4] I described an example of innovation that exemplified innovation-in-action. Geoff, an administrative officer in a local government authority I was consulting to several years ago, was concerned about the growing number of complaints he was receiving from members of the public about the length of time taken to get tombstone inscriptions completed in time for burials. The process then, was one where a relative of the deceased would draft the details to appear on the tombstone and send them in to the relevant council department; Geoff would eventually receive this information. He would then complete a draft copy and send this back to the relative for their approval. Once the member of the public had signed off on the wording and design, Geoff would then have the tombstone inscribed.

The appropriate mindset for performing the innovation role is one of improvement seldom settling for a service or process that is "good enough."

This process often took weeks to complete and naturally relatives of the deceased became upset at the length of time the procedure took, particularly when they wanted to conduct the funeral service. This method was cumbersome and required several checks back and forward between members of the public and Geoff, as the officer-in-charge. An entirely new approach was needed; continuous improvement was not the answer to this problem. The solution was to find a more innovative way of significantly reducing the timeframe this checking task took.

Geoff, having given this issue some careful consideration, came up with a process whereby the relative would complete the wording they wanted on the tombstone plaque online, in a relevant section of the council's website. The council could then do a draft immediately and send it back to the relative via email for checking. Once the relative was happy with the draft, Geoff's team would commence work. This reduced the process from three weeks to one week. This new approach is now common practice and illustrates the capacity to problem-solve and think critically about a workplace dilemma.

Table 9.1 illustrates ten KPIs for the element of problem-solving and critical thinking.

There are two competencies involved in these ten KPIs for the element of problem-solving and critical thinking. Some of the indicators relate to the general *capacity to solve problems*. The other indicators specifically relate

TABLE 9.1   KPIs for Problem-solving and critical thinking

Element: Problem-solving and critical thinking					
Key performance indicators	5	4	3	2	1
1. I have identified a number of practices and processes in my workplace that could be changed or improved.					
2. I can break down most workplace problems into detail.					
3. I can critically analyze the causes of most workplace problems I deal with.					
4. I can think of more than one instance where I have investigated and tested alternative ideas and approaches to workplace processes and practices in the interests of finding a better way.					
5. I consider myself to be very good at problem-solving in the workplace.					
6. I am capable of thinking through critically all the steps in sequence involved in a complicated process to do with my work.					
7. I know when to following standard operating procedures and when to use my initiative and creativity.					
8. I frequently come up with positive and helpful suggestions in meetings that can resolve a dilemma we are facing in the workplace.					
9. Sticking to the tried and proven solution is not necessarily the way I like to do things.					
10. I am always thinking critically about a better way of carrying out the work I do.					

to the *capacity to analyze complex situations*. Together, this set of KPIs explains problem-solving and critical thinking.

Customer responsiveness

Customer responsiveness involves an understanding of, and openness to, the customer and their needs. We all have customers, whether they are internal or external to the business. Customer responsiveness in essence means that everything said, thought about, and done ought to have the interests of the customer in mind. If our thought processes, communication, and actions always have the customer "front and center," we are by definition responsive to their needs.

At the heart of innovation and continuously improving the goods and services we produce and provide, is enhancing the customer experience. Providing a better customer experience can be achieved in any number of ways. But it all begins with an attitude of empathy for the customer and their circumstances.

More specifically, an employee competent in this element is able to identify, understand, build relationships with, and adapt to the requirements of external and internal customers. The employee who displays customer responsiveness does so in a measured way; reflecting the goals and values of the company they are employed by, and being fiscally responsible in the process. This element requires more than faithfully executing the company's standard processes, practices, and procedures. Employees need to be knowledgeable of – and responsive to – the constantly changing expectations of customers, focusing particularly on the quality and timeliness of the service they provide. This means the receptive employee is relentlessly trying to improve their approach and willing to adopt new methods when it's helpful to do so.

To illustrate my point, Southwest Airline's Senior Vice President for Corporate Communication, Ginger Hardage, told participants at a conference a story about a Southwest pilot after "September 11":

On September 11, 2001, after terrorists had brought "Twin Towers" down, all other planes that were already in the air were grounded. A Southwest plane was directed to land at an airport that Southwest did not serve, and the passengers and crew were put up in a hotel. When Southwest management called the hotel to enquire about the passengers and crew, they were told that no one was there – the pilot had taken everyone from that plane out to the movies. There's no manual from which to learn that, said Hardage. At Southwest, employees are encouraged to make decisions from the heart, and in turn, these proactive gestures provide positive benefits to the customers and the company.[5]

In a survey, 76 per cent of Americans think that a company's treatment of its employees is a major factor in whether customers will purchase from that company. As Southwest makes its employees the top priority, it is really demonstrating customer responsiveness.[6]

Table 9.2 summarizes ten KPIs for the element of customer responsiveness.

There are two competencies supporting these ten KPIs for customer responsiveness. The first competency has to do with an *awareness of the customer and their needs*. Second, several of the KPIs are related to the competency of *responding to customers and their needs*. Both competencies are crucial for performing customer responsiveness, the second element associated with the innovation and continuous improvement role.

In this chapter, we have looked at the essence of the innovation and continuous improvement role. This is the second of the two interpersonal non-job roles and the fourth and final non-job role covered in Part II. I have defined the role and explained its relevance and importance. Briefly, the two elements of the innovation and continuous improvement role are problem-solving and critical thinking, and customer responsiveness. Together, Tables 9.1 and 9.2 cover 20 KPIs relevant to this role.

This completes Part II of *The End of the Job Description*. Part III is concerned with the implementation of the role description in an organizational setting. Briefly, we cover some collaborative strategies for

TABLE 9.2   KPIs for Customer responsiveness

Element: Customer responsiveness					
Key performance indicators	5	4	3	2	1
1. I'm always thinking of how the work I do will impacts on the customer – whether they are internal or external to the organization.					
2. I often try to put myself in the shoes of my customers.					
3. I'm generally very responsive to the needs of my customers; they are my number one priority.					
4. I have offered several practical suggestions to my manager or colleagues on ways to improve our capacity to service the needs of customers.					
5. I always go out of my way to build constructive working relationships with those colleagues that rely on the work I do.					
6. I believe I fully understand all the challenges my customers face.					
7. I always try to balance the needs of the organization with those of my customers.					
8. I am always aware of the implications of what I do and how it will affect my internal and external customers.					
9. I am always interested to try new approaches to my work if I think it will positively impact on the internal or external customer.					
10. I am very open to the suggestions of my colleagues and customers about ways of doing things better and faster.					

converting job descriptions to role descriptions; how these four non-job roles can be evaluated; and finally, where the role description fits in the context of the organization's performance framework.

The **Top 10** Key Points …

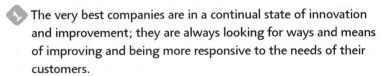

The very best companies are in a continual state of innovation and improvement; they are always looking for ways and means of improving and being more responsive to the needs of their customers.

2. To contribute to business improvement, employees need to think a certain way; for instance, never being entirely satisfied with the *status quo*, always looking for improvements. The innovation and continuous improvement role puts the spotlight squarely on the value and importance of this attitude.

3. A powerful growth and development inhibitor is the emphasis on compliance and conformity in the workplace. Most organizations are still locked into the stability and predictability mindset of the last century.

4. Beyond the work tasks embedded in the job description there are usually no KPIs around business improvement.

5. The employee has to embrace change and improvement; and it requires the manager to let go of their addiction to compliance and encourage constructive disobedience.

6. The role of innovation and continuous improvement is imperative; finding different and superior ways of approaching issues specific to the workplace is everyone's duty.

7. Continuous improvement, as the phrase implies, is progressively making improvements in the way things are currently being done. Innovation is about coming up with an entirely new way of doing something.

8. There are two essential elements that are important in exercising the innovation and continuous improvement role: problem-solving and critical thinking, and customer responsiveness.

9. Problem-solving and critical thinking is having the capacity to not only find solutions to challenging problems in the workplace but also being able to constructively think through these potential solutions.

10. Customer responsiveness involves an understanding of, and openness with, the customer and their needs.

part III

Implementing Role Descriptions

10

Strategies to Formulate Role Descriptions

As a general rule, people are not as inclined to embrace anything new unless they are consulted first. So I strongly suggest the employee has an input in modifying the KPIs to suit the work they do.

Bruce sat down with Mick, Keith, and Maggie in the meeting room to discuss the four non-job roles included in their new role description. The three employees were machine operators in a production company that manufactured springs for a wide variety of applications. They had the same job, but worked in different shifts in the company. Although the machine operators worked separately, they worked with several other machine operators in shifts. Bruce, the company's HR manager, wanted to gather a small team together to consider the four non-job roles and their application in the context of the operators' work.

Bruce had the lists of KPIs copied in preparation for the meeting and was intending to run through each element of the four non-job roles and their related KPIs. He was quite prepared to make modifications to the KPIs where necessary.

"Let's start with the positive mental attitude and enthusiasm role. The first KPI statement for the first element – solution-focus – reads, 'When

encountering an uncommon problem in my work, my first reaction is to consider some ways of resolving it.' So, what are some of these uncommon problems you face in your work, guys?" asked Bruce, opening the meeting confidently.

Mick was the first to speak: "Well sometimes we are given jobs to complete unexpectedly. These jobs are often out-of-the-blue and we have to make a decision about whether to complete what we are doing or move straight to the new job; it is a matter of working out priorities."

The other three operators nodded in agreement.

Bruce continued, "Should we include the word 'scheduling' in this KPI so that it is more relevant to the work you do? It would then read as follows, 'When encountering an uncommon scheduling problem in my work, my first reaction is to consider some ways of resolving it.'"

They all nodded in affirmation and Bruce moved on to the next KPI.

In Part III, we take a step back from the details of the non-job roles framework covered in Part II and consider three crucial issues in the implementation of role descriptions. These three matters are: Engaging others in the role description process; assessing non-job performance; and positioning the role description in the organization's performance framework. I'm hoping I can adequately address these three subjects to your satisfaction. By doing so, you should be ready to make a clean break from the job description and replace it with a role description – the third generation work document. I'm sure you appreciate by now that this step, done successfully, is at the core of changing the culture of an enterprise from a focus on the job to a focus on performance.

We start by considering several strategies for formulating role descriptions. I'm operating on the assumption that you already have in place reasonably well-documented job descriptions.

I repeat, this is not a book on the specifications of writing well-crafted KRAs, KPIs, and targets. There are plenty of books that do just that. If the job description is non-existent, poorly written, or inconclusive, you

have extra work to do. A poorly put-together job
description is not improved by merely attach-
ing the four non-job roles framework to it.
The job role dimension still needs to be
clear, precise, and up-to-date.

I hope you don't have even the
faintest impression that I think
the task-based dimension of work
is not vital. It is. To be clear, what I have
said is that the job description is incomplete
and doesn't reflect all the work performed in the
workplace. Much of this work, captured in the non-job roles framework,
should be included alongside the job-task dimension of performance in
the work document. But the non-job roles framework needs to be based
on the solid foundation of a clear, accurate, and current second generation job description, as we discussed in Chapter 1.

Instead of being another book on how to write a better job description,
The End of the Job Description is about a different work document with a
different emphasis; a third generation role description that better reflects
the totality of work in the workplace. So the book in your hands is
designed to help you retrofit the four non-job roles framework I discussed
in detail in Part II to the second generation job description.

Customizing KPIs

You may be thinking, "Okay I get that. But why can't I just take the model
literally from Part II and attach it to my current job description and call it
a role description?" You can. But there are two problems with that simple
approach. First, the four non-job roles are not specifically tailored to types
of work. I'm sure you recall me saying that the four non-job roles are valid
across all industries; and I stand by that statement. But these non-job
roles are more valid if the KPIs are customized for the work-at-hand. The
short vignette at the beginning of this chapter illustrates this point.

The KPI statements in Part II are general enough to be applicable to all forms of work; although many of these indicators can be tweaked to be more germane. Here are a couple of examples to add to one at the beginning of the chapter.

Take the career development role for instance. The two core elements – applicable to any employee in any industry – are *technical development* and *personal development*. In Table 8.1 (*see* page 144), the third KPI for the technical development element is expressed as: *I would describe myself as very coachable when shown how to do something new at work.*

For example, consider how this KPI could relate to a supervisor in a manufacturing environment; the KPI could be adapted to better reflect this work. This KPI might be changed to: *I would describe myself as very coachable when shown how to better supervise my team.* Or, consider the position of a technician, located in a confined laboratory. This KPI for the technical element of the career development role might be more aptly expressed as: *I would describe myself as very coachable when shown how to carry out my technical work in the laboratory.* These two modified statements reflect the work being done. Customization of the KPI strengthens its relevance for the incumbent, their boss, and colleagues.

The second important reason for adapting the KPIs to fit the work environment is to gain some commitment – and even enthusiasm – from the employee for the non-job role dimension of their work. As a general rule, people are not as inclined to embrace anything new unless they are consulted first. So I strongly suggest the employee has an input in modifying the KPIs to suit the work they do. If you decide not to collaborate with employees on this project, don't be surprised if there is widespread skepticism and a lack of engagement. The employee – without being consulted – may think the role description is simply another imposition foisted upon them from HR. Could we blame employees for thinking that?

What's more, the employee – familiar with the work they perform – will undoubtedly have some valuable input to offer. In most cases, the employee knows the work they do intimately; they are in a great position to customize the KPI statements. Collaborating with the person who actually does the work can be a source of great insight into how non-job roles can contribute to performance. Furthermore, what an employee does – and what they think they ought to do – can be explored. Briefly, the idea of working with employees to craft the role description is based on maximizing employee buy-in and tapping into their work knowledge.

In the following few pages, I have suggested several ways this can be done. Regardless of the method you use, the overriding purpose here is to produce a quality document that more completely captures work performance. And a vital ingredient of success is a high level of cooperation between the incumbent, their manager, and fellow employees, both functional and cross-functional. Applying role descriptions is an organization-wide project, involving everyone.

Let's now consider some methods for doing this.

Dynamic duo method

Using this approach, the manager selects two employees who perform the same role. In collaboration, they consider the non-job elements, competencies, and KPIs in the context of the work they do. For example, two accounts receivable clerks have identical tasks they perform. Following a discussion between the manager and both clerks, KPIs are modified based on their first-hand experience of how they carry out their work from a non-job perspective. Using this method, the manager or supervisor works in partnership with the two employees to review their non-job roles.

The *dynamic duo* method can be used even where there are several people employed to do the same work. Instead of taking six accounts receivable clerks off the "floor" at once, the manager could select two experienced and high-performing employees to customize the KPIs.

Team method

With the *team* method, the manager chooses three or four individuals who make up a homogeneous team (similar to the scenario at the beginning of the chapter), all of whom perform the same tasks, to review the non-job roles framework. This method is particularly useful when a job role has many incumbents, or when the role can be found in several departments or across several work shifts.

As an example, there may be a works' supervisor in six geographic locations in the same organization, all basically doing the same work. The manager of these supervisors can bring all six together and, as a team, work through the KPIs in the role description. This method ensures that all members of the team are given the opportunity to have some input into the development of the role description.

However, I have a word of caution when using this method. Teams should be kept small and manageable; groups larger than six employees often have difficulty reaching consensus; they will inevitably be slower to review the KPIs. Should a team be larger than six people, it might be best to use the dynamic duo method.

Supervisor–incumbent method

As the name suggests, the *supervisor–incumbent* method is the supervisor or manager working with a single employee to analyze the four non-job roles. The supervisor–incumbent method is particularly effective in certain situations. For instance, it works effectively when an employee is new to the role, and they are the only person employed to do that work in the company. A collaborative approach in this case can align the expectations of the manager and new employee. A new employee is likely to be impressionable and keen to start on the right footing. By discussing these KPIs, the manager and employee can agree upon performance standards and expectations in the non-job (and job) dimension of work.

Another possible situation for applying the supervisor–incumbent method is when there are managerial concerns about an established employee and areas of their performance. This misalignment may be attributable to a lack of understanding on the part of the employee of their organizational role. These misunderstandings could be due to a number of other factors too, such as major and sudden changes to the employee's job role.

Single employee method

The *single employee* method means the employee, or the manager, completes the document on their own. For specialized work roles with only one employee, or for a vacant/new position, this may be the only method available. But in any case, it obviously can't be done collaboratively. For this reason, it is the least preferred method. If it is possible, a review of the role by the manager in concert with the employee can still have some merit; it can clarify expectations between the two.

The process I have just described – using any of the methods outlined above – is referred to as a role analysis. A thorough role analysis is a critical first step in adopting role descriptions instead of job descriptions. A systematic appraisal of the non-job dimensions of the role description is similar to a job analysis.

Role analysis

A *role analysis* is defined as the process of collecting, analyzing, and recording information about the requirements of a role in order to provide the basis for a role description. In the context of the non-job roles framework, a role analysis focuses on the demands made on the role-holder in terms of their non-job dimension of work. As we've discussed, this investigation is best done collaboratively with employees occupying those roles; working together they collect, analyze, and record the necessary information for the role description.

The key purpose of conducting a role analysis is to reliably and accurately define the requirements and expectations of the non-job roles. Done thoroughly and cooperatively, a role analysis provides accurate and agreed upon KPIs. This information is then used in a variety of HR practices, including recruiting and selecting candidates, and assessing and managing performance. We covered other HR practices in detail in Chapter 2 that will be influenced by a role analysis.

A job analysis, as distinct from a role analysis, is based exclusively on the job dimension of one's work. A comprehensive role analysis, like the role description, covers both the job and non-job roles of work.

A T   T H E   C O A L   F A C E   ...

Role analysis conversations

Employees need to be clear about their roles, responsibilities, and accountabilities in the workplace. The role description should be the starting point for this clarity. But regardless of how well the role description is formulated, it doesn't guarantee understanding. Each employee needs to discover what is required and how to apply their knowledge, skills, and attitude to the various roles they perform. When this match between the person and the roles they perform occurs, a good role-fit has been achieved.

Regular conversations between the employee and their manager provide a good avenue to explore the "role-in-reality" and compare it to the written document. These conversations can build a robust shared understanding of expectations between the manager and employee. Specifically, some of the work-related opportunities and challenges can be discussed and addressed in these conversations. Knowing they have their manager's support, the employee can feel confident demonstrating initiative consistent with organizational priorities. Briefly, role conversations can empower employees to act in the "right" way, in the "right" circumstances.

Regular role conversations throughout an organization align roles and people. In most cases, these conversations improve role clarity in the minds of both manager and employee. Role clarity means the employee is crystal clear on what is expected of them and can perform with the confidence that their behavior in their job and non-job roles – in most cases – is consistent with their boss's perspective.

These role conversations are hugely underestimated in my view; they are a powerful tool for improving organizational performance.

Building upon the various methods of formulating role descriptions, here are several guidelines for completing role analyses you might find helpful:

- Providing training for those involved in the process of analyzing and evaluating non-job roles.
- Agreeing on a role description format, specific to the needs of the organization, and written to enable work roles to be assessed to a common standard.
- Distributing a list of the generic KPIs for each element of the non-job roles framework (covered in Part II) to the role analysts so they can facilitate their customization.
- Removing gender, race, and individual identification from the role description.

This is not an exhaustive list of considerations. But it does serve as a useful starting point. The important overarching advice here is to treat this exercise as an important workplace project. It needs methodical planning so that it maximizes positive impact throughout the organization.

Once job descriptions have been converted to role descriptions, it is important for managers to sit down with their team members and discuss the implications of these changes. These conversations, as I mentioned earlier, are not to be taken too lightly. They ought to be a priority. Time needs to be allocated to discuss these changes. Here are some useful questions to facilitate these role conversations:

• How can each of the four non-job roles be performed to add value?
• What do the KPIs mean for organizational performance?
• How can the manager best lead and support team members to perform the elements and KPIs of the non-job roles?
• What, if any, concerns do team members have about performing the four non-job roles?
• How will these non-job roles be assessed objectively (we cover a methodology in the next chapter)?

Again, this is not a definitive list of questions or considerations. But it is a useful starting point for role analysis conversations. These conversations support the development of the role description and therefore further advance the significance of the non-job performance dimension of work.

In the next chapter, we look at the assessment methodology I propose for determining the extent to which these four non-job roles are being performed.

The **Top 10** Key Points …

1 The role description needs a solid foundation. A clear, accurate, and current second generation job description is that foundation.

2 The KPI statements in Part II are general enough to be applicable in any form of work. Although some of these statements can be tweaked to be more germane.

3 An important reason for adapting the KPIs to fit the work environment is so that employees enthusiastically embrace the non-job role dimension of their work.

4. Using the dynamic duo method, the manager or supervisor selects two employees who perform the same role; they consider the non-job elements and KPIs in the context of this role.

5. With the team method, the manager or supervisor chooses three or four individuals who make up a homogeneous team, all of whom perform the same tasks, to complete the document.

6. As the name suggests, the supervisor–incumbent method is the supervisor or manager working with a single employee to complete the role documentation.

7. The single employee method allows for the employee or the manager of the role to complete the document on their own.

8. A role analysis is defined as the process of collecting, analyzing, and recording information about the requirements of a role in order to provide the basis for a role description.

9. The key purpose of conducting a role analysis is to reliably and accurately define the requirements and expectations of the job and non-job roles.

10. Once job descriptions have been converted to role descriptions, it is important for managers to sit down with their team members and discuss the implications of these changes.

Assessing Non-Job Performance: A Case Study

> The role of the manager is to hold up a mirror for the employee to look at themselves and, in particular, the way they are viewed by others.

"Julie, you mentioned to me the other day that you didn't want to go on that project management training course. Is there any particular reason for that?" asked Sandra, Julie's boss. "I'm too old to learn anything new, Sandra. Besides, I don't want to take up space that can be used by someone else; one of the younger team members would get more out of it than me," came Julie's reply.

"Julie, I don't buy that. You are never too old to learn. As you are aware, career development is important. I know you are at the end of your career, but ... I need you to think differently about this. I need you to be open to continually growing and developing for your own benefit, and for the benefit of the company," Sandra challenged Julie.

"But Sandra, I would be taking up space for one of the younger team members and I'd feel guilty about that," Julie protested. "Julie, you are not stopping someone else from going on that workshop, I promise you. You have no need to feel guilty. I strongly believe it will benefit you and that's why I have nominated you to go," said Sandra, with an assertive tone of voice.

180

In this chapter, I will outline a process for assessing the performance of the four non-job roles. The best way to bring this process to life is through a case study. I will refer to "Michael." Michael's non-job roles were "assessed" using a multi-source feedback methodology. "Terry," Michael's manager, sat down with Michael to discuss the feedback. Action plans were developed to improve aspects of Michael's non-job performance, specifically related to performing the team role.

I'd suggest using this process I am about to describe annually. This method can be done either manually or electronically, depending on your preference. I refer to this approach as the "non-job performance conversation process."

Non-job performance conversation process

The *non-job performance conversation process* consists of five interrelated steps. I'll run through the five steps first. Once I have done that, I will apply the process to the case of Michael so that you can see how it works in practice. The process is reliant on *multi-source feedback*; that is, feedback on the KPIs from three distinct sources. Although I acknowledge that there are critics of multi-source feedback, it has been widely and extensively used successfully in the western world for over 25 years.

Multi-source feedback is growing in popularity. The multi-source methodology is more commonly referred to as *360-degree feedback*; it is most often used for management development and coaching. Despite its critics, the main strength of multi-source feedback – as the name suggests – is that data is drawn from more than one source; in this case, three sources. The three sources in this process are: Employee (self-image); their manager (management-image); and at least four colleagues (team-image).

All three inputs are based on observations; the three sources are asked for their perceptions. In this process, the statements used for the sources to respond to are the non-job role KPIs I have covered in Part II. Although people's observations or perceptions are subjective judgments, these perceptions are – as the saying goes – "reality in the eye of the beholder." These observations are collected and collated in a non-job roles multi-source feedback report that provides the manager and employee with a foundation for a performance conversation.

A T T H E C O A L F A C E ...

Flush with cash: Saving fuel costs

History of 360-degree feedback

The German military first began gathering feedback from multiple sources in order to evaluate performance during World War II. Others also explored the use of multi-rater feedback during this time period via the concept of T-groups.

One of the earliest recorded uses of surveys to gather information about employees occurred in the 1950s at Esso Research and Engineering Company. From there, the idea of 360-degree feedback gained momentum, and by the 1990s most human resource and organization development professionals understood the concept. The problem was that collecting and collating the feedback demanded a paper-based effort including either complex manual calculations or lengthy delays. The first led to despair on the part of practitioners; the second to a gradual erosion of commitment by recipients.

However, due to the rise of the Internet and the ability to conduct evaluations online with surveys, multi-rater feedback use steadily increased in popularity. Today, studies suggest that over one-third of US companies use some type of multi-source feedback. Others claim that this estimate is closer to 90 per cent of all Fortune 500 firms. In recent years, Internet-based services have become standard in corporate development, with a growing menu of useful features (such as multi languages, comparative reporting, and aggregate reporting).[1]

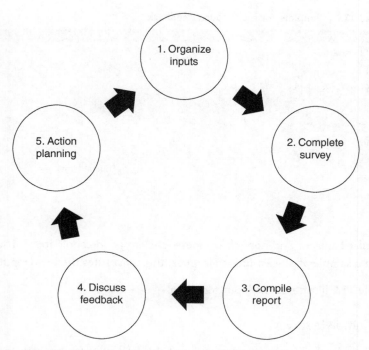

FIGURE 11.1 Non-job performance conversation process

Figure 11.1 illustrates the five steps involved in the non-job performance conversation process.

Allow me to briefly explain each of the five steps in the process.

1. Organize inputs

The first step in the process is to decide on the sample to provide input on the employee's non-job role performance. The first of the three sources of input is the employee themselves. The manager of that employee is the second input. These two inputs are a given in this process. A third source of input comes from the employee's work colleagues. Colleagues or team members who are in a position to observe first-hand the employee's

TABLE 11.1 Template for multi-source feedback

Input Source	Name	Number of Inputs
Self Perspective		
Self		One
Manager Perspective		
Manager		One
Team Perspective		
Team		
Team		Four, at least.
Team		
Team		

regular behavior and non-job competencies are good candidates. I'd suggest a sample of at least four colleagues; this constitutes the team input.

Table 11.1 illustrates the input template.

2. Complete survey

Each individual earmarked as an input, based upon the template from Table 11.1, receives an email invitation to complete the survey online. The four or more participants representing the team perspective are allocated a unique key to protect the confidentiality of their responses. This is important. For the data to be meaningful, the team members should feel comfortable expressing their honest opinion. This is more likely to occur on the understanding that their input can't be traced back to them. Although there is no guarantee that someone will always express a truthful view, making the respondent anonymous helps, from my experience.

A link in the email invitation takes the participant to a secure website to complete the survey. There are 110 statements to complete. These statements are the KPIs for the elements of the four non-job roles. In other words, the statements are taken from Tables 6.1, 6.2, 6.3, 7.1, 7.2, 7.3, 7.4, 8.1, 8.2, 9.1, and 9.2 in Part II. There are ten KPI statements for each of the 11 elements. From past practice, it should take no more than 20 minutes for a participant to complete the survey.

The participant has three choices for each statement; they can *agree*, *disagree*, or *neither agree nor disagree* with each statement. You will note that the KPIs in the above-mentioned tables have a rating scale from one to five (five being high and one low). The five-scale rating system may be more applicable if you are doing this manually. There is also provision at the end of the online survey to volunteer a comment.

3. Compile report

The six or more inputs collectively produce a report. The report is broken down into four sections, one for each of the non-job roles. In the system I use, the results are illustrated in three ways. There is an overall graphic for each element, showing the aggregate level of congruence (agreement) or incongruence (disagreement) between the three perspectives mentioned earlier (see Figure 11.2).

For instance, at one end of the spectrum, you could have the employee, their boss, and four colleagues all in total agreement about one or more KPIs. This agreement can be either positive or negative. As an example, all six inputs can agree that Joe Blow is a good (positive agreement) or poor (negative agreement) listener. At the other end of the spectrum, it is possible that the aggregate results for the three perspectives could be incongruent. For instance, Joe Blow could think that he is a good listener; their manager thinks he is a poor listener; and the aggregate team result neither agrees nor disagrees on the same KPI. There are a range of possible reasons for this alignment or misalignment of perspectives; this can be explored in the subsequent non-job performance conversation.

The second graphic is a histogram illustrating the aggregate outcome of each perspective for each element (see Figure 11.3). This data is identical to the first graphic just mentioned; it is just illustrated differently. And finally, each statement is represented with statistics indicating the range of responses for each KPI (see Tables 11.2 and 11.3). In other words, the statistical data shows the number and percentage of respondents who agree, disagree, or neither agree nor disagree with the KPI.

4. Discuss feedback

The non-job roles multi-source feedback report is the channel for a conversation between manager and employee. This is a performance conversation with the focus squarely on the non-job dimension of work. It is during this conversation that perspectives are shared, incidents discussed, expectations aligned, and action plans developed.

Here are several questions the manager should ask the employee during this conversation to start a conversation:

- What is your overall impression of the feedback?
- What feedback are you particularly pleased with?
- What areas surprised you? Why did they surprise you?
- What are two key messages you got from the results? What are you going to do about these messages?
- What can I do to better support you in any of these non-job areas?

You will notice that these questions are open-ended and non-judgmental. The objective of this performance conversation is to get the employee to reflect on their feedback in a way that is constructive and practical. The emphasis of the conversation is on development, not assessment.

5. Action planning

Action planning is the final key step in the non-job performance conversation process. The plan is to build upon the strengths and work at overcoming, or minimizing, the weaknesses in the report. The process works best when the employee arrives at their own conclusions from the feedback and subsequently develops their own action plan.

By arriving at their own developmental plan, the employee is taking responsibility for their learning. The plan will be to either start behaving, stop behaving, or modify the way they are behaving in

By arriving at their own developmental plan, the employee is taking responsibility for their learning.

their non-job roles. For example, the change for the employee could be to exhibit more solution-focused behavior by thinking through several courses-of-action or options to a problem before raising it with their manager. Then again, the key message from the report may be a general theme covering several elements. For example, there might be an overall message to the employee to listen more attentively to colleagues. The plan in this case would be to pause for a moment and to practice active listening without pre-judging the contribution of others. Action plans ought to be regularly followed-up by the manager.

I'd like to put this non-job performance conversation process into context, particularly the last two steps. We will consider Michael's feedback and the accompanying conversation with Terry, his manager.

Case study

Michael is a warehouse manager in a large distribution center. He manages ten employees in the warehouse. Michael has great industry knowledge, extensive work experience, and superior technical skills; he has worked in warehousing for 15 years. Michael's job role involves the planning, management, and distribution of customer product orders in a busy environment. It's a big job.

Michael's boss, Terry, is very happy with the work Michael does for the company. But Terry has some reservations about Michael's performance in teams. The report confirms some of Terry's concerns with Michael's non-job performance.

With the support of HR, Terry put forward the names of four colleagues in the team of ten representing the team perspective. Six people, including Michael and Terry, competed the survey online. The confidentiality of the four team members was protected with the issuing of unique keys to access the online survey. The report was collated and Terry prepared for his non-job performance conversation with Michael.

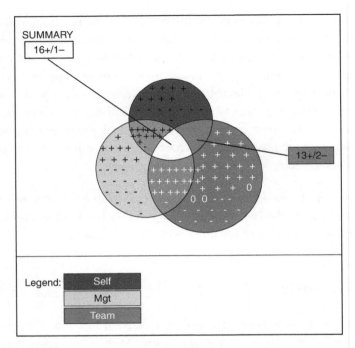

FIGURE 11.2 / Summary 1 of non-job performance report

Figure 11.2 shows the overall summary of data from Michael's report in one of two formats.

As a quick explanation of this graphic, the three circles represent the three perspectives: Self-image; management-image (Mgt); and team-image. Figure 11.2 illustrates the level of agreement between the three perspectives. The overlapping areas between two or three circles (white space in the center) show the overall extent of agreement. Agreement between perspectives can be either positive or negative. Positive and negative agreement is represented as a + or − sign in the graphic. The more + and − signs in the overlapping areas, the more agreement between two or more perspectives.[2]

Another way this data is represented is shown in Figure 11.3

The three bars represent the aggregate result for each of the three perspectives. As you can see from the legend, the aggregate result is a combination

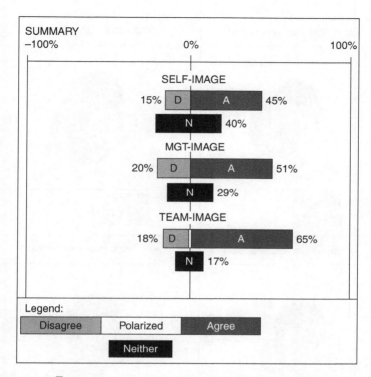

FIGURE 11.3 Summary 2 of non-job performance report

of disagree; polarized; agree; and neither responses. A polarized result means there is a relatively even split view between an aggregate agree and disagree response in one perspective. In Michael's case, it is barely visible in the team-image. Overall, an employee and their manager would prefer a relatively higher percentage of agree responses than anything else.

Figure 11.4 is the collection of summaries of Michael's results for the four elements of the team role.

The reason I am illustrating Michael's team role summaries here is that this is the area where his boss has some concerns. More specifically, Terry honed in on two KPIs and their results in the report. The two results reinforcing Terry's pre-survey view are represented in Tables 11.2 and 11.3.

Team Role - communication	Team Role - accountability
Legend: Self / Mgt / Team	Legend: Self / Mgt / Team
Team Role - collaboration	Team Role - leadership
Legend: Self / Mgt / Team	Legend: Self / Mgt / Team

FIGURE 11.4 Summary 3 of the elements of the team role

TABLE 11.2 Statistics for a leadership element KPI

Team Role: Leadership

Q5 *I am an active and constructive contributor in team meetings.*
Self: Agree
Mgt: Neither
Team: Agree   *Agree*:   50% (2/4)
                Neither: 50% (2/4)
                Disagree: 0% (0/4)

TABLE 11.3 Statistics for a communication element KPI

Team Role: Communication

Q11 *I generally listen carefully to what others are saying.*
Self: Disagree
Mgt: Neither
Team: Polarized *Agree*:   50% (2/4)
                 Neither: 0% (0/4)
                 Disagree: 50% (2/4)

Before studying the non-job performance conversation between Michael and Terry, allow me to briefly explain the make-up of these two tables. First, notice from the headers, these two KPIs are associated with two different elements of the team role, namely, *leadership* and *communication*. Second, Q5 and Q11 indicate the order of the KPI statements in the randomized survey. Third, the statement in these tables is what Michael responded to. Terry and the four team members responded to this similar statement: *He is an active and constructive contributor in team meetings* and *He generally listens carefully to what others are saying.* Fourth, notice on the left-hand side of the tables, Michael's aggregate team result is listed both as a percentage and numerical breakdown. These two results consumed most of the conversation between Michael and Terry.

Turning now to the interpretation of these two results, Table 11.2 can be read like this: Michael thinks he is an active and constructive contributor to team meetings (self-image); but Terry (management-image) is undecided. Moreover, Terry has observed Michael contributing constructively in team meetings sometimes. Although at other times, he observed Michael's input as destructive – or at the very least, unhelpful – hence, his neither response. Two of the team share Terry's view; they record a neither response. Michael's other two colleagues were more positive and recorded an agree response.

In response to the statement, *I generally listen carefully to what others are saying*, in Table 11.3, Michael disagreed. Terry said neither; and the aggregate team response was polarized, meaning two observed Michael listening carefully to what others had to say and two had the opposite view. Both KPIs are related; they're about demonstrating respect for others in the workplace. These results suggest Michael could do more to show deference for others he works with.

Here below is part of the conversation between Michael and Terry discussing these two results:

"Michael, what do you make of the results for the statement, *I am an active and constructive contributor in team meetings*?" Terry asks. "I think I always try to be constructive when we have our team meetings, Terry. I'm a bit surprised about yours and the two team members' responses. Three of you sat on the fence on that statement," Michael replies.

"Michael, sometimes you can be very constructive in team meetings. For example, last week you raised that matter about monitoring your team's lifting technique in the warehouse. I thought that was constructive since we were talking about safe work practices at the time. But on other occasions, I think you are so eager to jump in and have your say that sometimes your colleagues may not believe you're listening to them. If we look at the results for the statement, *I generally listen carefully to what others are saying*; two team members disagreed with that statement. What do you think, Michael?"

"Well, sometimes I do get impatient and too eager to respond. Maybe some people think this means I am not listening or not being constructive? Maybe I need to take a deep breath, be patient, and listen until my team mates have finished what they want to say," says Michael fruitfully. "I think that's a fair observation, Michael. Can I get your commitment that you will take that deep breath and bite your tongue next time you want to jump in and say your piece?" Terry asks confidently, looking directly at Michael.

"Yes, Terry, I'll give it a go; I don't mean to come across as destructive or not listening," is Michael's reassuring response.

"Okay then, let's record that as part of your action plan and we can have a look at the results next time for these KPIs, to determine whether there has been any change," Terry concludes, wrapping up this part of their conversation.

I want to reiterate an important point here: The critical aspect of the non-job performance conversation process is the performance conversation, not the report. The report is nonetheless the catalyst for a productive conversation. This process is about developing the employee; it is not about assessing, rating, or categorizing them.

The manager's role in this performance conversation is to facilitate a discussion with the employee. Furthermore, it is about inviting the employee to reflect on the results of the survey in a constructive and non-defensive way; to gain their commitment to improve or change things that need changing. Just as importantly, the conversation should be about reinforcing the positive messages too.

The analogy I often use to illustrate the role of the manager in this process is this: The manager's role is to hold up a mirror for the employee to look at themselves and, in particular, the way they are viewed by others. The report is the mirror. The manager's responsibility is to invite the employee to self-reflect and comment on what they see in the mirror. Continuing the analogy: How can the image in the mirror be improved and what can I do to support you? These are two questions the manager ought to focus on in this conversation. The important final piece of the conversation is gaining commitment from the employee that they will modify their behavior from that point on.

In the final chapter, we'll look at the role description and where it is situated in the performance framework of an organization.

The **Top 10** Key Points …

1. The non-job performance conversation process involves five steps.
2. The first step in the process is to decide on the sample of invitees to give input for the employee.
3. The second step is that each individual earmarked as an input receives an email invitation to complete the survey online.
4. The third step is the production of a non-job roles multi-source feedback report.

5. The fourth step is a conversation between manager and employee about the report. The objective of this performance conversation is to get the employee to reflect on their feedback in a way that is constructive and practical.

6. Action planning is the final key step in the non-job performance conversation process.

7. The non-job role report is broken down into 11 sections, one for each element of the non-job roles framework.

8. The case study between Michael (employee) and Terry (manager) illustrated steps four and five: the performance conversation and the action plan respectively.

9. The most critical aspect of the non-job performance conversation process is the conversation, not the report. The report is the catalyst for a productive conversation.

10. The important final piece of the conversation is gaining commitment from the employee that they will modify their behavior from that point on.

chapter 12

The Performance Management Framework

> The performance management framework ... has application in any organization, whether it is from the public or private sector, large or small, professional or blue collar, or a mix of both.

I vividly recall how incredibly easy my coaching conversation with Terry was. I was sitting in the managing director's office of QTK, a dealer for transport refrigeration and transit air conditioning products. I wanted to formulate a vision, mission, and set of core values for the business. I thought this process might take several agonizing hours; it normally does! I was dead wrong about that. Terry had all the answers on the tip of his tongue; I just had to ask the right questions. Terry's responses were very impressive. My job was to prize the information from Terry's head and express it on paper.

Sitting in his office, I started our coaching conversation with this question: "For your business to be even more successful, Terry, than it currently is, what would that look like?" "I want this business to be the premier dealership in the country," Terry confidently replied, without a moment's hesitation. "Okay Terry, that sounds like a vision statement right there: To

*be the premier dealership in Australia," I suggested with some encour-
agement. "I'm happy with that Tim; it sums it up pretty well, I think,"
affirmed Terry.*

*"How does QTK get there? What does the business need to do?" I asked
with some traction. "Well, I think we have to provide excellent products
and service that our customers want." "What does that mean, Terry?" I
jumped in for clarification. "That means on-time delivery, providing value
for money, and superior all-round service," said Terry with conviction.*

*"Let me summarize. QTK's mission is this: 'By providing products and
services that meet requirements, are delivered on time, and are priced to
provide superior value.' How does that sound?" I said. "Good, I like it. In
our industry that is what it is all about," Terry replied.*

*"How will we achieve this, Terry? What are the core values that employ-
ees need to exhibit to make this happen?" "Well obviously the first one
is customer satisfaction. If we don't demonstrate this, we simply won't
become the premier dealership in the country."*

"Okay, what else is important?"

*"As a business, we need to be more reliable than we currently are. People
need to be able to depend on us. I think we need a culture of continuous improvement. And I need all my employees engaged and involved
in this vision," claimed Terry. "So the four values I heard from you then
were: 'customer satisfaction', 'reliability', 'continuous improvement', and
'employee participation and growth,'" I paraphrased, trying to sum up the
conversation at this point.*

"Sounds good to me."

*Like I said earlier, I couldn't believe how easy this process was and how
clear Terry was about the business's direction. I had no doubt he'd achieve
this vision, over time. His next step was to consult widely in the business
to get maximum buy-in for this.*

As I discussed in Chapter 2, the job description is the pillar supporting
all HR practices in a business. To be effective, most HR processes and

procedures depend upon a well-documented job description. Specifically, the job description gives pointers on where to look in the marketplace to recruit suitably qualified and experienced people. The job description guides the selection process to find the most suitable recruit for the position it describes. It helps in evaluating the relative strengths and weaknesses of a host of potential candidates; their competencies, skills, qualifications, and experience can be weighed up against the job specification. The document explains what tasks the new employee is expected to perform. The job description orientates the new recruit and shapes their induction into the business. It is used to assess and develop the job-holder's training and development needs.

After the probationary period, the job description determines how the employee's performance is reviewed, and the outcome of that review. Performance reviews directly or indirectly influence remuneration decisions, rewards, and possibly remediation. The job description is used to justify dismissing employees. The KRAs in the job description form the basis of succession planning decisions. For decades, the job description has been omnipotent in HRM.

Despite its power, employees and employers are often dissatisfied with the way the job description is constructed. We know it doesn't capture the full extent of work performance, particularly non-job performance. While I'm not advocating throwing away the work document, I want to challenge our obsession with a focus on the job. I'm questioning our conventional idea of performance being tied to a job of work. What about the idea of non-job performance? How can we elevate the legitimacy of non-job performance? In essence, these are the questions I'm interested in.

We know the job description is generally poorly written. But the problem is deeper than good crafting. Organizational work is nothing like what it was a 100, or even 50, years ago. Yet we still persevere with an out-of-date format that doesn't comprehensively reflect performance in a post-industrial, knowledge-sharing, rapidly changing modern workplace.

Although the format of the job description has changed, its change is nowhere near as transformational as work itself. For the past 50 years, HR practitioners have grappled with the following questions:

- What is the right balance between task-based and person-based information contained in the job description?
- What competencies do we include (and exclude) in the job description?
- What happens when the job inevitably changes? How and when are these changes captured in the job description?
- We recognize that non-job competencies are important. How do we include them in the job description, which is fundamentally job-focused?

These issues have plagued us for decades. These questions have not been adequately dealt with. So it is understandable why there is malaise about the job description. To add to this disquiet, we rely heavily on it; the job description forms the foundation of all HRM practices. This is the rationale for the role description replacing the job description.

In this final chapter, I want to position the role description in the context of organizational performance. This chapter introduces you to the *performance management framework*. In terms of its position in the framework, the role description has a bigger part to play than the job description. The role description is more inclusive; it incorporates several of these missing elements of work performance, characterized as non-job roles.

Even with the advancement of shifting from first to second generation formats, the job description still doesn't comprehensively cover work performance. Although there is a relationship between the job description and other HRM practices, as we have discussed in Chapter 2, the document is often not developed as a component of the performance management framework. The "dots are not always connected."

For instance, it is not always apparent how the description of the job moves the business closer to achieving its vision or mission. It is with this common shortcoming that I want to connect the dots and explain the relationship between the common parts of the performance framework. In doing so, I want to make sure that the role description doesn't suffer the same fate of separation as the job description often does from the performance management framework.

The performance management framework is illustrated in Figure 12.1. I will refer to each part of this framework throughout the chapter. More specifically, I will discuss each component part and illustrate its link to other parts of the framework.

The performance management framework I am about to define in more detail has application in any organization, whether it is in the public or private sector, large or small, professional or blue collar, or a mix of both.

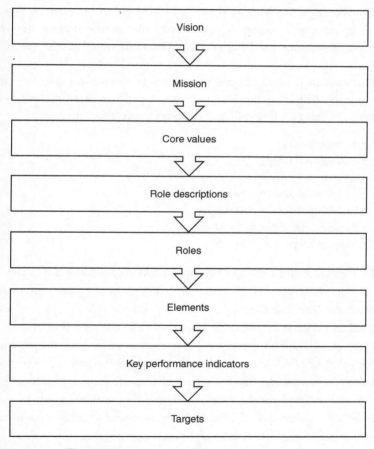

FIGURE 12.1 Performance management framework

Observing the framework in Figure 12.1, you'll notice that one of the eight component parts is the role description. I'll subsequently explain the significance of the role description in the framework, and how it differentiates itself from the job description.

The framework explains the linkages between these eight parts essential for managing performance in an organization. Briefly, working our way from top to bottom, the *Vision* is a broad statement of the direction the business wants to head in. It responds to the question: *What is our aspired future for the business?* For example, Bill Gates' vision for Microsoft was originally: *To have a personal computer on every desk running Microsoft.* The *Mission* is a broad statement of how the business intends to achieve its vision. It responds to the question: *How* are we going to achieve our vision? For example, Dell Computers' mission reads:

> Our mission is to be the most successful IT systems company in the world by delivering the best customer experience in all markets we serve. In doing so, Dell will meet customer expectations of:
>
> - highest quality;
> - leading technology;
> - competitive pricing;
> - individual and company accountability;
> - best-in-class service and support;
> - flexible customization capability; and
> - superior corporate citizenship.[1]

The *Core Values* express the key behaviors needed to achieve the mission. For example: *Respect – which means we put the needs of our customers above all else.* The *Role Descriptions* identify the five *Roles* employees are expected to perform to assist the business to achieve its vision, mission, and core values. The *Elements* are the key result areas for both the job and non-job roles. *Key Performance Indicators* (KPIs) are the way the elements are assessed. *Targets* identify the standard of performance expected for each KPI. Once the elements, KPIs, and targets for job and non-job behaviors have been "nailed down," valid and reliable reward structures ought to be put in place to reinforce these sought-after performance standards.

QTK performance framework

Following on from the vignette at the beginning of the chapter, here is the outcome of the conversation and extensive consultation with organizational members; illustrated are the first three steps in the performance management framework: the vision, mission, and core values of QTK.

Vision

To be the premier dealership in Australia.

Mission

By providing products and services that meet requirements, are delivered on time, and are priced to provide superior value. This will be achieved through customer satisfaction, reliability, process improvement, and employee participation and growth.

Core Values

Customer Satisfaction

This means courteous attention, value for money, and timely service.

Reliability

This means quality products and consistency of service.

Process Improvement

This means continually striving for improvement in everything we do.

Employee Participation and Growth

This means that all employees of QTK are given the opportunity to grow and develop within the business.[2]

Let's now take a closer look at each of the component parts in the framework.

Vision

I like to use the common coat hanger found in most people's closet as a metaphor for the vision. We all have too many coat hangers, right? They seem like they breed! They are pretty much useless on their own; coat hangers can even be downright annoying. So too, a vision statement hanging on a wall can be annoying; no one pays the statement much serious attention and it normally just takes up space that could be used for other purposes.

However, the coat hanger is very useful for hanging garments off. Moreover, the coat hanger helps to shape the item of clothing hanging from it. This is what a vision statement does when employees are emotionally attached to it. Ideally everything that is said, done, and thought about in an organization should be consistent with the vision.

The way we approach our work; the way we treat each other, and our important stakeholders and customers; the way we problem-solve; the way we reward each other; the way we measure our success and so on, should be consistent with the vision statement. The vision is there to guide and inform every decision made by all organizational members, regardless of their position.

In addition, a compelling vision has four features. It should:

- Inspire.
- Challenge.
- Inform.
- Instigate.

A vision must be inspirational to some degree. *To provide the very best customer service* is hardly likely to get employees out of bed excited to come to work in the morning! The challenge of the vision should be "out of reach, but not unreachable"; in other words, it needs to test organizational members. A vision needs to inform; it responds to the question: *Where are we heading?* You've no doubt seen vision statements extend to one or two pages in length. A powerful vision can be captured in one simple sentence. The best vision statements are straightforward; they aren't complicated. And finally, the vision should be a call-to-action; it should instigate a certain type of activity. Everything that happens (or doesn't happen) in an enterprise ought to move the business closer – directly or indirectly – towards realizing the vision.

Consider these famous vision statements:

- *Give me liberty or give me death*
  – Patrick Henry, United States Revolutionary War Leader, 1776.
- *We shall never surrender*
  – Winston Churchill, British Prime Minister, 1941.
- *By the end of the decade, we will put a man on the moon*
  – John F. Kennedy, United States President, 1962.
- *A computer on every desk and in every home*
  – Bill Gates, Microsoft Chairman and Chief Executive Officer, 1980.

None of these statements are complicated; the general idea is to keep it simple and clear.

Mission

A vision encapsulates *where* the organization is heading and the mission statement explains *how* this will be attained. Like vision statements, mission statements are often too long and too detailed; again, simplicity and clarity are key.

An organization's mission statement is the opportunity to define the company's goals, ethics, culture, and norms for decision-making. According to Tim Berry, founder and Chairman of Palo Alto Software and

Bplans.com, the best mission statements describe a company's goals in at least three dimensions:

- What the company does for its customers.
- What it does for its employees.
- What it does for its owners.

Berry points out that some of the best mission statements also extend themselves to include a fourth and fifth dimension: What the company does for its community, and for the world.[3]

Here is an example of a gas station's mission statement, based upon this vision: *To be the number one choice of motorists for stopovers on Highway 310*:

> Our mission is to offer commuters on Highway 310 competitive gas prices and great food. The company will make a healthy profit for its owners and provide a rewarding work environment for its employees.

So, to summarize, the mission is how the vision will be achieved.

Core values

To recap: A vision is *where* we are heading. The mission is *how* we'll get there, and the values are the *appropriate behaviors* for success. Like the vision and mission, managers and employees are frequently cynical about the organization's values statement; it can be viewed as a meaningless collection of words. The emptiness of the value statement is due in large part to it being put together by the CEO or senior management, without widespread consultation. If the majority of organizational members haven't been invited to have their say,

A vision is where we are heading. The mission is how we'll get there, and the values are the appropriate behaviors for success.

it shouldn't be surprising that they feel no ownership or connection with the values.

Apart from no consultation, another problem embedding a set of values into the cuture of an organization is the inappropriate behavior of senior leaders. The people who wrote the values statement – or at least those who are considered the vanguard of the values – don't always act in accordance with the stated values. Worse still, the behavior of leaders can be contrary to the values. I'm sure you've witnessed disparity between the behavior of the leaders and the stated values. Not having input in developing the values and frequently witnessing leadership behavior that is contrary to the ideal behaviors inevitably results in detachment and cynicism.

Yet another reason corporate values are looked upon with skepticism is that – apart from being displayed on a wall plaque – they're no where to be seen. The values are out of sight and therefore out of mind. For instance, the majority of job descriptions I have seen make no reference to the organization's set of values and how they relate to the job of work. And because the values aren't mentioned in the job description – or are mentioned superficially – they are not really discussed and reviewed at performance appraisal time, or any other time. Without reference to the values, they are consequently "seen" as having no relevance to the work being done.

Another big mistake is having too many values. I think four is fine. Any more. than four values and people get confused; they forget what the values are, and how they apply in their day-to-day working life. Deciding on the four core values is an exercise in priorities. The key question ought to be: *What are the top four values needed to reach the vision?* Selecting four values isn't implying that other values are irrelevant; it's just that the four values identified in the statement are paramount for achieving the strategic direction.

To be relevant, values need to be defined. Take the value of *respect*, for example. My definition of respect could be entirely different to yours. If the meaning of respect – or any value – is not spelt out, it is merely a label or slogan, with no real application. An accompanying statement, such as *Respect means always having the customer as our number one priority*, helps to bring the value to life.

Assessing values is problematic. Although values are certainly tricky to quantify, you and I have definite opinions about whether they have been enacted or violated. For instance, we are capable of judging whether someone is being respectful or disrespectful, particulary given a definition of respect. We may not agree, but we are likely to be certain in our own mind.

I like the idea of assessing the core values annually, with all organizational members being invited to participate in that evaluation process. A survey collectively evaluates the leader's behaviors in relation to the core values of the business. Giving everyone the opportunity to participate in a survey is a democratic process for assessing the values-in-practice. The annual core values survey I have designed evaluates how closely they are aligned to the behaviors of organizational members and provides a set of benchmarks for a comparative analysis.[4]

Role descriptions

Now that we know *where* we are heading (vision), *how* we'll get their (mission), and *what* work behaviors we need to do so (core values), we move to the role description. In the context of the performance management framework, the role description signifies how the five roles can be performed to reach the vision. This book is essentially about the role description, so I needn't say much here.

But the role description plays a more prominent part in the performance management framework than a job description. This is largely because the role description considers two dimensions of work: The job and non-job dimension. The job description has traditionally focused on one dimension of work: The job dimension. Taking into account a broader interpretation of performance, the role description strengthens its relevance in the framework.

Roles

Again, I won't say too much about the roles in the framework; most of it has already been said in Part II. In the non-job roles framework, there are four roles: Two personal and two interpersonal. This means that everyone within the business is expected to perform five roles: One job role and four non-job roles. The job description has been too heavily focused on the job role, and non-job competencies have consequently been under-valued. This diminishing of non-task behaviors unintentionally weakens organizational performance. Non-job roles should have a legitimate place in the performance management framework.

Elements

We've also covered the 11 elements associated with the four non-job roles framework in Part II. The two terms *Elements* and *Key Result Areas* (KRAs) essentially explain the same thing. KRAs however, usually cover the broad clusters of task-related activities of a job. In simple terms, KRAs can be defined as the primary responsibilities of a job-holder; that is, the core areas of accountability relating to that job.

Although the focus of the KRAs is on the job role, they are nevertheless important for several reasons. First, they are used to set goals and objectives for the person holding that position. Second, KRAs help to prioritize activities and therefore improve the job-holder's management of their time and themselves. Third, they clarify the various task-clusters associated with the position. Fourth, by listing a set of KRAs, the emphasis is on results or outcomes rather than activity. Fifth, they can – but often don't – help to make a clear connection between the job responsibilities and the vision, mission, and core values of the organization. And finally, KPAs define the job role's purpose to others within the business. These five reasons are why KRAs are a valuable characteristic of the job description.

But the significant downside of KRAs is that they are task-centric; they don't take into account non-task-specific result areas required to be a high-performing organizational member. More specifically, KRAs rarely say anything about the responsibility of the role-holder to be enthusiastic and positive; working in teams; committing to their growth and development; and a preparedness to contribute to improving the workplace. As undeniably crucial these aspects of work are to organizational performance, KRAs don't cover them.

For this reason, I have used the term *elements* instead of *KRAs* in the performance management framework. Further, I think the concept of the element can be applied to task-related activity in the same way as the KRA. So in my performance management framework, elements refers to both the job or non-job dimensions of work. As we covered in Part II, there are 11 non-job elements. The number of elements for the job role will vary depending on the position. But to summarize, the elements in the framework are specific areas of activity that are related to all five job and non-job roles.

Key performance indicators

KPIs are the gauges used to determine how the elements (or KRAs) will be measured in performance terms. Despite the common error, KPIs are not the measurement themselves; they are the method of how the element will be measured. In the job role, for instance, an element (KRA) for an office-based role may be *Administration*, the KPI measurement might be timeliness and accuracy. One KPI could be to meet deadlines on submitting reports. Or, another KPI for this element might be to ensure that all documentation is completed error-free. In both cases, a target can be set to indicate an acceptable level of performance.

The KPI or method of assessment can either be qualitative (process) or quantitative (number). Many KPIs can't be measured as a number. For instance, *Customer Service* may be an element of the job role. For this element, the KPI might be best expressed as adhering to a specific process or procedure when dealing with the customer. But for a sales role, the KPI might be expressed as a number in terms of sales results. Briefly, there are only two ways of expressing a KPI: either as a number or process.

/ Targets

The final component of the performance management framework is the targets. Targets are the actual benchmark for successful performance; again, they cover KPIs for both job and non-job roles. For example, referring back to the job role of *Administration*, the KPI could be either timeliness or error-rate. So a realistic target may be to meet 100 per cent of all predetermined deadlines. Or, the target could be that all completed documentation has no more than 5 per cent of grammatical or spelling errors, or better still is 100 per cent free-of-mistakes. For other KPIs that can't be quantified, the target is following a particular process, with no deviation, such as sticking to a pre-set ordering procedure.

One of the main reasons we favor numbers is their simplicity, clarity, and perceived objectivity. This bias towards quantitative data and analysis in organizational life means managers frequently shy away from putting targets on qualitiative KPIs. So, without a clear target, these less tangible KPIs of work are usually considered less important. What's more, without a clear indicator, managers are disinclined to give perfomance feedback. But with a little thought and planning, all desirable workplace tasks and behaviors can be distilled into a neat process or procedure, if they can't be quantified. At the very least, carving out a process or procedure sets specific and clear guidelines for employees to follow.

Of course people will have differing intepretations of workplace behavior that can't be measured numerically. But that is not – in my view – a valid reason to avoid setting a target. Paradoxically, when desirable workplace behavior is difficult to measure objectively, this is all the more reason to set a target. Why? Target-setting adds clarity around performance expectations. In a tricky situation, open to differing interpretations of perfor-mance, the manager and employee ought to discuss this situation, either before or after the occurance. A constructive performance conversation can lead to better mutual understanding and elucidation.

By taking on the non-job performance conversation process covered in the previous chapter, targets can be set numerically for all non-job KPIs

TABLE 12.1   Statistics for two technical development KPIs

Career Development Role: Technical Development		

Q79 *Continuously improving and upgrading my skills-set is a priority for me.*
Self: Neither
Mgt: Neither
Team: Disagree *Agree:*
                      Neither:
                      Disagree:
	25% (2/4)
	25% (0/4)
	50% (2/4)	

Q84 *I have discussed my opportunities for growth and ways of enhancing my skills in those areas with my boss.*
Self: Neither
Mgt: Neither
Team: Agree *Agree:*
                      Neither:
                      Disagree:
	50% (2/4)
	25% (1/4)
	25% (1/4)	

from the multi-source feedback report. For example, consider the results in Table 12.1 for the element of technical development.

These results for two KPIs clearly show some room for improvement in technical development, an element of the career development role. For the KPI for Q79, *Continuously improving and upgrading my skills-set is a priority for me,* I would suggest a reasonable target to strive for over the next year might be for the "self-image" and "management-image" to *agree* with this statement, and three out of four "team-image" participants to change their opinion to *agree*.

In Q84, based on the following KPI: *I have discussed my opportunities for growth and ways of enhancing my skills in those areas with my boss*, there is also scope for improvement. I would – at the very least – expect the employee and manager to be able to agree on this statement next time. These targets for Q79 and Q84 can be set, assuming both the manager and employee agree. So you can see it is possible to set numeric targets for the KPIs of elements of the non-job roles using this multi-source feedback approach.

In conclusion, I have attempted to show the relationship between the various component parts of the performance management framework. Ultimately, there should be a link between all targets and the vision statement. The role description's place in an organization's performance framework is more substantial than the second generation job description, which is fixated on job-related activity. The role description shifts the focus from the job to performance.

Instead of one job role, the role description involves four additional non-job roles. Doing away with the outdated term, "key result area" with its job-specific bias, I suggest replacing it with the term, "element," covering both job and non-job roles. Using multi-source feedback, quatitative targets can be set for non-job KPIs. All-in-all, the role description strengthens the work document and its impact on the performance management framework.

This brings us to the end. I hope you've enjoyed reading my book as much as I have enjoyed writing it. In sum, Part I was primarily about arguing that the job description, despite its evolution, is fundamentally unsuitable for documenting contemporary organizational work. Work now is a world apart from the Ford motor car assembly line of the early 20th century. But the way we document the work people are supposed to accomplish has not kept pace with the transformation of work. Tinkering at the edges – as many HR professionals are doing – is not the answer. The job description is holding employees and organizations back from realizing their full potential.

In Part II, we covered the non-job roles framework. I have argued for the inclusion of four roles that make up the framework; they are critical aspects of work performance, albeit, non-job performance. The four roles were broken down into 11 elements and 110 KPIs.

Finally, in Part III we covered implementation strategies for the role description. Briefly, we covered strategies to formulate role descriptions, how these non-job roles can be assessed, and where the role description fits in the performance management framework.

The **Top 10** Key Points ...

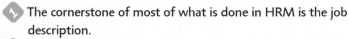

1. The cornerstone of most of what is done in HRM is the job description.
2. In terms of positioning in the performance management framework, the job description and role description are the same. But the role

description is more comprehensive; it incorporates many of the missing aspects of performing at work.

 The framework explains the linkages between eight parts essential for managing performance in an organization.

4. The vision is a broad statement of the direction the business is heading. It responds to the question: What is our aspired future for the business?

5. The mission is a broad statement of how the business intends to achieve its vision. It responds to the question: How are we going to achieve our vision?

6. The core values express the key behaviors needed for the achievement of the vision.

7. The role description identifies the five roles employees are expected to perform to assist the business achieve its vision, mission, and core values.

8. The elements are the KRAs for both the job and non-job roles.

9. Targets identify the standard of performance expected for each KPI.

10. Ultimately, there should be a link between set targets and the vision.

Notes and References

1 Role Descriptions: The Next Generation

1. S. Castellano (2014) "What's in a job?," *Training & Development*, January.
2. E. Eyre: "Frederick Taylor and Scientific Management: Understanding Taylorism and Early Management Theory," http://www.mindtools.com/pages/article/newTMM_Taylor.htm.
3. J. S. Schippmann, R. A. Ash, M. Battista, L. Carr, L. D. Evde, B. Hesketh, and J. I. Sanchez (2000) "The practice of competency modeling," *Personnel Psychology*, 53 (3), pp. 703–40.
4. W. Bridges (1994) "The end of the job," *Fortune*, September, pp. 50–7.
5. Charles Woodruffe (1993) "What is meant by a competency?," *Leadership & Organization Development Journal*, 14 (1), pp. 29–36.
6. R. D. Goffin and D. E. Woycheshin (2006) "An empirical method of determining employee competencies/KSAOs from task based job analysis," *Military Psychology*, 18 (2), pp. 121–30;
   F. Lievens, J. I. Sanchez, and W. DeCorte (2004) "Easing the inferential leap in competency modelling: The effects of task-related information and subject matter expertise," *Personnel Psychology*, 57 (4), pp. 881–904;
   K. Soderquist, A. Papalexandris, G. Ioannou, and G. Prastacos (2010) "From task-based to competency-based: A typology and process supporting a critical HRM transition," *Personnel Review*, 39 (3), pp. 325–46.
7. http://www.tlnt.com/2013/11/18/whats-wrong-with-the-job-description-anyway/.
8. Hewitt Associates (2005) "Research highlights: How the top 20 companies grow great leaders." Retrieved from http://www.inspireimagineinnovate.com/pdf/Top_Companies_2005_report.pdf.

2   The Harmful Impact of the Job Description on HRM

1. Adapted from T. Baker and A. Warren (2015) *Conversations at Work: Promoting a Culture of Conversation in the Changing Workplace* (London: Palgrave Macmillan).
2. N. Bennett and G. J. Lemoine (2014) "What VUCA really means for you." Retrieved from https://hbr.org/2014/01/what-vuca-really-means-for-you.
3. T. B. Baker (2013) *The End of the Performance Review: A New Approach to Appraising Employee Performance* (London: Palgrave Macmillan).
4. Outdoor Pursuits Centre (2008) "History of OPC." At http://www.opc.org.nz. Accessed January 2014.
5. This refers to The Five Conversations Framework, a substitute for the standard performance review process. Data from the five conversations is captured online and available for analysis.
6. Baker (2013) *The End of the Performance Review*.

3   The Job Description and the Old Contract

1. T. B. Baker (2014) *Attracting and Retaining Talent: Becoming an Employer of Choice* (London: Palgrave Macmillan).
2. T. B. Baker (2009) *The 8 Values of Highly Productive Companies: Creating wealth from a new employment relationship* (Brisbane: Australian Academic Press).
3. Ibid.
4. This research is based on Baker's doctoral thesis. His thesis is entitled, "Towards a new employment relationship model: Merging the changing needs and interests of individual and organisation." At http://eprints.qut.edu.au/16064/.

4   The Job Description and the New Contract

1. Adapted from K. Cole (2005) *Management Theory and Practice*, 3rd edition (French's Forest, Sydney: Pearson Education Australia).
2. T. B. Baker (2009) *The 8 Values of Highly Productive Companies: Creating wealth from a new employment relationship* (Brisbane: Australian Academic Press).
3. R. M. Kanter (1995) "Mastering change," in S. Chawla and J. Renesch (eds) *Learning Organizations: Developing cultures for tomorrow's workplace* (Portland, OR: Productivity Press), pp. 71–83.
4. "WTF is a hackathon?" Retrieved from https://medium.com/hackathons-anonymous/wtf-is-a-hackathon-92668579601.

5 The Non-Job Roles Framework

1. Adapted from K. Cole (2010) *Management: Theory and Practice* (French's Forest: Pearson Australia).
2. http://blog.readytomanage.com/top-10-most-valued-job-skills/.
3. T. B. Baker (2009) *The 8 Values of a Highly Productive Company: Creating Wealth from a New Employment Relationship* (Brisbane: Australian Academic Press).

6 The Positive Mental Attitude and Enthusiasm Role

1. Adapted from T. B. Baker (2015) *The New Influencing Toolkit: Capabilities for Communicating with Influence* (London: Palgrave Macmillan).

7 The Team Role

1. Adapted from T. B. Baker (2014) *Attracting and Retaining Talent: Becoming an Employer of Choice* (London: Palgrave Macmillan).

8 The Career Development Role

1. Adapted from K. Cole (2010) *Management: Theory and Practice,* 4th edition (French's Forest: Pearson Australia).
2. D. T. Hall (2004) "The protean career: A quarter-century journey," *Journal of Vocational Behavior,* 65, pp. 1–13.
3. W. S. Chin and R. M. Rasdi (2014) "Protean career development: Exploring the individuals, organizational and job-related factors," *Asian Social Science Journal,* 10, p. 21.
4. C. Orpen (1994) "The effects of organizational and individual career management on career success," *International Journal of Manpower,* 15(1), pp. 27–37.
5. Skills Australia (2012) "Better use of skills, better outcomes: Australian case studies." Retrieved 16 March 2015 from http://www.industry.gov.au/skills/Publications/Documents/Better-use-of-skills-Case-study-booklet-8-May-2012.pdf.
6. T. B. Baker (2014) *Attracting and Retaining Talent: Becoming an Employer of Choice* (London: Palgrave Macmillan).

9   The Innovation and Continuous Improvement Role

1. http://www.illumine.co.uk/2013/05/examples-of-innovation-in-the-workplace/.
2. The author is unsure as to whom the original term of "constructive disobedience" is attributable.
3. http://www.mirror.co.uk/news/uk-news/flush-with-cash-british-airways-saves-740383.
4. T. B. Baker (2013) *The End of the Performance Review: A New Approach to Appraising Employee Performance* (London: Palgrave Macmillan).
5. United States Chamber of Commerce (2008) "Southwest's secret to a positive corporate culture: its employees." Retrieved June 24, 2008 from http://www.uschamber.com/bclc/profiles/southwest.htm.
6. Ibid.

11   Assessing Non-Job Performance: A Case Study

1. http://en.wikipedia.org/wiki/360-degree_feedback.
2. For more information on these graphics, see http://www.hipsys.com or contact the author tim@winnersatwork.com.au.

12   The Performance Management Framework

1. http://www.strategicmanagementinsight.com/mission-statements/dell-mission-statement.html.
2. T. B. Baker (2013) *The End of the Performance Review: A New Approach to Appraising Employee Performance.* (London: Palgrave Macmillan).
3. http://articles.bplans.com/writing-a-mission-statement/.
4. I can be contacted at tim@winnersatwork.com.au for more information on implementing an annual values survey.

Index

Printed and bound in Great Britain by
CPI Group (UK) Ltd, Croydon, CR0 4YY